BRINGING IT ALL BACK HOME

The influence of Irish music at home and overseas

Bringing It All Back Home

*The influence of Irish music
at home and overseas*

SECOND EDITION

Nuala O'Connor

MERLIN

PUBLISHING

Published in 2001 by

Merlin Publishing
16 Upper Pembroke Street
Dublin 2
Ireland

www.merlin-publishing.com

ISBN 1–903582–03–2

A CIP catalogue record for this book is available from the British Library.

Typeset by Carrigboy Typesetting Services, County Cork
Printed by Leinster Leader Ltd

Acknowledgments

I would like to express my thanks to all those who helped me in the researching and writing of this book, but first and always to Philip King, whose idea it was to make *Bringing It All Back Home*.

I am also greatly in the debt of Nicholas Carolan, Director of the Irish Traditional Music Archive, who read the original manuscript, made corrections and suggested changes, and also to Sadhbh Nic Ionraic, also of the Irish Traditional Music Archive.

To Jackie Small, Harry Bradshaw, Peter Browne, Jean Ritchie, George Pickow, Helen Davis, Judy Murray, Bairbre Ní Fhloinn, Geraldine O'Reilly, Mick Moloney, Rionach Uí Ógáin, and Ciarán and Mary Rowsome Buíochas Mór.

To the hundreds of musicians mentioned in the book and the thousands who are not, I am profoundly grateful. Fad Saoil Agaibh.

Contents

One

The Dawning of the Day

I have a theory that soul music originally came from Scotland and Ireland.

VAN MORRISON

Bringing It All Back Home was a five-part documentary film series about Irish music broadcast by the BBC and the Irish television network, RTÉ, in 1991. The series traced the journey of Irish traditional music from its earliest recorded history to the present day and explored the ways in which it adapted to changing circumstances, mainly brought about by Ireland's unique history of colonial occupation and emigration.

"Emigration," one Irish historian noted, "is a mirror in which Ireland sees itself reflected." Emigration and Irish music are inextricably bound together. Both tell stories of exile, displacement, resilience, and a fierce identification with Ireland. The emigrant's need to retain a sense of Irish identity, while problematic in many ways, effectively ensured the survival of Irish traditional music. The experience of emigration, viewed as exile by many, was for others a liberation from poverty and oppression. For those who remained at home, emigration created ambivalent feelings of guilt and loss. The experience of emigration also influenced Irish music culture, enriched it, and acted as a force for renewal and inspiration.

The music recorded for the series attests to the Irish experience of emigration. An ongoing negotiation between the known and the unfamiliar, the old and the new, change and continuity characterises Irish traditional music. This constant flux, encompassing the encounter in the eighteenth century between the old harp music of the Gaelic aristocracy and the European art-music of the new English ruling class, reflects a friction between the loss of a culture and the need to adapt. Traditional music which travelled to America and Britain in the hands and heads of Irish emigrants interacted with the music it found there.

Irish traditional music, then as now, was primarily dance music, jigs, reels, and hornpipes, played by rural working people for communal celebrations and events, such as fairs, weddings, wakes, and so on. In the case of America, Irish traditional music and song merged on the Appalachian frontier with other indigenous music to form American folk music, and further south with the music of black slaves to influence the blues. Traditional dance tunes, airs and songs went into the melting pot.

In America, a new country, rapid change was the driving force. Irish music absorbed the spirit of the new age in order to reinvent itself and meet the musical needs of the New World.

The twentieth-century influences of media and technology sent Irish music off in many different directions, towards rock, country, pop, electric folk, blues and the avant-garde. Collections of the music of the past have also played a part in revitalising contemporary Irish music, particularly the classical tradition.

What came through in the making of the series was that all of these Irish musical forms share common features, not necessarily of musical construction, but of spirit, which identify them as Irish.

Through the music that has touched all of these generations, we can read the history of Ireland and her people, especially her emigrant people. The traditional music of Ireland was the only enduring cultural baggage that impoverished emigrants could take out of the country. In the past one hundred and fifty years Ireland has had more of its people leave the country than remain in it. This is unique in the history of emigration.

Being Irish outside Ireland is central to the Irish life experience. The question of identity for Irish people is fraught with ambivalence and tensions. Bono's famous words "I never saw myself as Irish until I went to America" resonate for many Irish people who have lived abroad.

Tensions come in the form of contradictory pressures – one to become assimilated into the new country, the other to affirm and retain Irishness.

Irish traditional music evolved through this process, unrecognisably transformed in some situations, hardly changing at all in others. In places here and there, often on opposite sides of the globe, Irish music remained as it always was: a living, vibrant connection to centuries of tradition. Music also returned to Ireland in many guises at different times, reinvigorating the tradition when it most needed it, "bringing it all back home" to the source and sensibility from which it sprang.

Irish Music . . . Soul Music

Mícheál Ó Súilleabháin, composer, performer and Professor of Music at the University of Limerick, warns against analysing traditional music without reference to performance. What makes Irish music unique is the people who make the music:

> The most important thing in music is the technique of making it and at the heart of the creative process itself – the thing at the heart of the music making – is something which is in the fingers or in the throat technique of the singer.

He further identifies Ireland's until recently peripheral position in Europe – half in the first world, half in the third world, not fully industrialised, predominantly rural – as the most significant determinant in the evolution of Irish music. Add to this the fact that Ireland was colonised for eight hundred years, during which time Gaelic culture and language were almost totally wiped out.

We're linked directly . . . here in Ireland into modern audio-visual technology and yet we have this older rural tradition existing in the cities. It's transferred from the country into the city, and instead of actually losing its heart, it started to find something, and it's almost like it's coming home.

Traditional Music

There are several definitions of the term "traditional music", all of which bear connotations of oral transmission. In other words, traditional music is passed on by mouth and by ear, not by written word or musical notation. The music is learned from the performances of other singers and players and one generation learns from the next in this manner. As Mícheál Ó Súilleabháin has said:

> Traditional music has to come out of an actual meeting of bodies in space, you know, people communicating; and I think it always has that immediacy and root and warmth as a result.

Ireland is unique in the western world in still retaining a vigorous, orally transmitted music. This "warm" musical atmosphere exerts an influence on musicians working outside the purely traditional field. There is still traditional music which has remained uncorrupted by other forms and idioms. It is not a museum piece. It is alive and developing, and attracts growing numbers of young musicians – an encouraging index of health. However, like many countries in the developed world, the pace of change has accelerated beyond the capacity of many social institutions to adapt. The overwhelming consumerism of western societies and the breakdown of old forms of interaction, such as community music, make for challenging times ahead for traditional music.

On the subject of definitions, the term "folk" music is often used interchangeably with the term "traditional" music. However, the two are not necessarily one and the same. In addition to having a folk music tradition which can be described as "music of the people", Ireland also has two other highly developed musical forms. One of these, the harping tradition, now defunct, was never folk music. The second, the "Sean Nós" tradition, drew some of its elements from the mediaeval bardic poetry that was the preserve of a scholarly élite. These forms are as complex and sophisticated as classical or European art-music. In their highest forms of expression, they are inaccessible to many performers and listeners.

Another characteristic of traditional music is anonymity. There were, and are, composers, but the nature of the music and the performance of it are such that the composer, even if known, was of little significance. The inexorable movement towards professionalism amongst traditional players and the extensive commercial exploitation of traditional music have changed this utterly. What is now known as "intellectual property" did not apply until recently to traditional music. Not alone can musicians rightly claim copyright for their own compositions but they can also claim it for their arrangements of existing traditional tunes.

The traditional tune itself operates only as melodic outline. As a bare melody, it is incomplete. The degree of variation and ornamentation that occurs in traditional music performance is its defining characteristic. The execution of the music is heavily dependent on the skill and creative imagination of the player, so within the actual performance itself there is an element of controlled extemporisation. In this way, each time a player plays a tune, he plays it as if it were for the first time. Each time he plays it, then, it will differ very subtly from the last time. In this way it is rather like jazz.

There is, however, a defined musical structure within which this extemporisation is allowed to take place. It is the mastery of this, in addition to imagination and skill, which combine to produce a great player. The player is thus both performer and composer. A player who attempts to move outside this structure, and there have been some, will not be able to play with other players. The nature of the transmission and performance of the music would work against this happening because Irish traditional music involves a community of musicians. A large part of the ethos of Irish traditional playing comes from musicians playing together in session for each other and for the listening community.

Gigs and paid concert performances were until very recently a small part of the picture because very few traditional musicians in Ireland made a living out of playing. The very idea of a professional traditional musician in the concert performance sense was considered unusual. An intrinsic part of the tradition was that there was no audience as we understand it in the modern sense; that is, passive recipients or consumers of music. Although this is no longer the prevailing mode in traditional music culture, there are elements of it still alive in the large numbers of amateur practitioners and in the enduring practice of session playing between professionals and amateurs.

The Origins of Traditional Music

The traditional music of Ireland as we know it today cannot be classified as "ancient". We do know, though, that music had an important place in ancient Ireland, important enough to be mentioned in an Irish mythological account of the origins of the three categories of Irish music: the "suantraí" (lullabies), the "geantraí" (joyful airs), and the "goltraí" (laments). These categories are literary inventions and do not represent any actual classification of Irish music. Significantly, a central role in the fable is ascribed to a musical instrument, a harp, which has magical powers. Although there is evidence that there were a number of musical instruments in use in ancient Ireland, the harp had pride of place.

The harper was the most elevated of Irish musicians. A feature of Irish society until the demise of the old Gaelic order in the seventeenth century, the harp has retained a symbolic pre-eminence, if not a musical one. It is the national emblem on Irish coinage. It is also the logo for Guinness stout.

Because of the oral nature of traditional music, we have no idea what this ancient music sounded like. The thread which joined Irish music to its past was largely severed in the seventeenth century, a period which also saw the beginning of the documentation and notation of Irish music.

The harping tradition did not survive beyond the eighteenth century. It was an oral tradition and the only way of reconstructing it is by way of eighteenth-century transcriptions of music collected from the last few harpers then still playing.

There is no doubt, though, that some Irish musical forms, particularly the "Sean Nós" singing tradition, have an ancient past. "Sean Nós", in Irish, means the "old style".

If we were to look at the important elements which went into the making of Irish traditional music we would see, first of all, an ancient Gaelic culture located on the very edge of Europe, more or less unaffected by the imperial predations of the Roman Empire. This culture was assimilated somewhat uneasily into Christianity, maintaining its distinctive features until Norman and then English colonisation began to erode it.

The national repertoire, as it is today, is rooted in the popular music of the seventeenth and eighteenth centuries. It consists of instrumental music, mostly dance music and airs, but also songs in Irish and English, and the musical remnants of the harping tradition of the old Gaelic aristocratic order.

A beautiful example of this kind of air is "A Stór mo Chroí" played by uilleann piper Liam O'Flynn and recorded for *Bringing It All Back Home*. Also recorded for the series was the song version, sung by the sisters Sarah and Rita Keane, of Caherlistrane, County Galway, in the west of Ireland.

Sisters Sarah and Rita Keane, traditional singers from County Galway, with their niece, singer Dolores Keane (left).

Instrumental Music

Most Irish traditional instrumental music played today is dance music. In the sixties, seventies and eighties it was more usually played for listening audiences than for dancers. Why this is so will be explained later, in Chapter Five. Since the set dance revival of the mid-eighties and the phenomenon of "Riverdance", the profile of all kinds of traditional dancing has risen in Ireland and outside of the country.

The majority of tunes in a traditional player's repertoire is comprised of reels, jigs, and (depending on their particular regional style, background, learning experience, or taste) of hornpipes, polkas, slides, mazurkas, and highlands. An increase in the numbers of professional players, foreign travel, an extensive festival circuit, and other factors has led to younger musicians including non-Irish traditional music in their repertoires.

In addition, some musicians, although not all, will on occasion play airs and song airs (the instrumental versions of songs) as solo pieces. These airs are often referred to as "slow airs" to differentiate them from the rhythmic dance music which is more usually played.

The traditionally trained uilleann piper Davy Spillane successfully modernised the slow air, using pipes, low whistle and accompaniment (including electric guitar) in his composition "Equinox". He achieved the same mood and ambience of the slow air. There can be no doubt that the source of inspiration for this haunting, ethereal piece of music was deep in the melodic conventions of the playing of airs.

There is one other small category of instrumental music, but one of ancient lineage: marching tunes. Clan marches came under interdict in the seventeenth century. They were considered to be seditious because of their association with the old Gaelic aristocracy. Fortunately, some of them were retained in the repertoire and were adapted as double jigs for dance music. The harper Máire Ní Chathasaigh recorded one such tune for *Bringing It All Back Home*. It's now a jig called "Humours of Ballyloughlin".

Dance Music

Dance music can be broken down into roughly seven or eight dance forms. (These are described in Chapter Five). An authoritative traditional music scholar, the late Breandán Breathnach, estimated as recently as 1985 that the national repertoire of reels, jigs and hornpipes stood at over six thousand individual pieces, with hundreds more tunes for different kinds of dances like polkas, sets, half sets and so on. It's important to understand that these are living tunes, not tunes which have been collected and noted by folklorists. They are in the repertoire of living, practising musicians. This repertoire is not a static thing.

The traditional music world responds to the vagaries of fashion as much as pop or rock music. Different dances are designated by their particular time signature (metre or beats to the bar). The unifying principle of the dance music in performance is known as the "round". The round is described by Mícheál Ó Súilleabháin as "not a theoretical concept . . . but a feeling of main pulses". It consists of a thirty-two-bar formula, or thirty-two "main pulses", within which there are usually two strains or "parts" of eight bars. Each of these is repeated – "doubled", in traditional music parlance – to make a total of thirty-two bars. This usually makes up the tune, which is repeated once again from the beginning and followed directly by another tune, played in such a way that one flows effortlessly into the other. To the untutored ear it is not always apparent that two tunes have been played. Listening and/or playing are two ways of recognising the structure and appreciating the subtleties of the music.

As always, there are exceptions. The parts may be played more than twice, or there may be more than two parts or strains in the tune. However, the whole will always be broken down into units of eight bars.

About these "main pulses" Mícheál Ó Súilleabháin says: "You can actually feel them move through your body, and you can see them going through the musician's body, if you watch the body movement, which is very important in all kinds of music." Once one is aware of this principle, one quickly becomes aware of main pulses in the playing. Understanding it adds immeasurably to the enjoyment of the music.

If you listen, for example, to the recording of Mary Bergin playing on tin whistle the reels "The Blackberry Blossom" and "Lucky in Love", you will notice that she adheres to the standard formula as outlined above. She plays the first strain twice, then the second strain twice, a total of thirty-two bars; she then repeats the whole tune again, making another thirty-two, and then segues straight into the second reel, "Lucky in Love", which is played the same way.

"The Blackberry Blossom" is played by Irish fiddler Paddy Glackin with two American virtuoso country fiddlers, Mark O'Connor and country-music star Ricky Skaggs. Having played the first part twice, instead of going into the second part of "The Blackberry Blossom", they play the first part twice again, making a thirty-two-bar exposition of the first part of the tune. The second part of the tune is doubled twice also. Then they return to the beginning and do it all over again, before going on into the second reel, "The Saint Anne's". Their version is exactly twice the length of Mary Bergin's version, but they remain within the eight-bar-unit formula.

A traditional Irish fiddler meets a traditional Appalachian musician: Paddy Glackin and American country music star Ricky Scaggs.

Ornamentation and Variation

Ornamentation and variation lie at the heart of all traditional playing and singing. It is through variation, embellishment, and ornamentation that the musician expresses his or her technical skill, imaginative powers, mastery of the form and, ultimately, personality.

It would be unthinkable in classical music to alter the musical text of, say, a Beethoven piano sonata. It must be played as written. The melody line cannot be changed at the discretion of the player; the time signature cannot stray from that designated by the composer; and so on. In traditional music the opposite is the case. The melody is only a framework, a skeleton that gets its flesh and character from the musicians who play it. This will be different each time it is played, though it will never change to the point where it is unrecognisable. These differences are subtle; the deeper the acquaintance the listener has with the music, the more they become apparent. The melody will always be the melody, a reel a reel and a jig a jig, and the tune will always operate within its own particular conventions.

To variation and ornamentation add intonation and style. These are the treasured qualities which make the tradition so rich and so immensely varied.

Singing

Two obvious divisions exist in Irish traditional singing – songs in the Irish language and songs in English – and two distinctive styles exist to go with them. Generally speaking, the singing style in Irish is the older of the two. The English singing style is based on the ballad, which is particular to English-language songs common to both England and America. With the exception of some mediaeval examples of Ossianic lays (lyrics or poems sung) in Irish no longer in the living tradition, there are hardly any ballads in the Irish language. There are Irish influences in the English ballads sung in Ireland and an Irish style of singing ballads, but the root is English.

Songs in Irish

With the long, slow decline of the Irish language went much of the music of that culture. In this process the song tradition was more vulnerable than the instrumental music. Not having an existence independent of the language as the instrumental music did, it could not accommodate such radical change. Breandán Breathnach, in *Folk Music and Dances of Ireland*, wrote:

> The decline of the language involved the rejection of the body of folk-song which had its existence in it. Strangely enough the associated airs were also discarded almost in toto.

While fragments of song airs or, indeed, of instrumental music became absorbed into the new repertoire, they were merely "sustained like particles of matter in a stream" and have not been identified in any systematic way; their age and provenance, as Breathnach stated, is a matter for speculation only. Fortunately, the Irish language and its song culture, although still endangered, did not disappear altogether. The country still has a store of songs in Irish and Irish-speaking singers to sing them. These "native speakers", so called because they come from those parts of Ireland known as the "Gaeltacht" where Irish is the first language, sing in the Sean Nós or old style (see Chapter Eight). They sing both Irish and English songs in this manner. There are also songs in Irish which are not sung in the Sean Nós style, but these are of more recent origin. Describing this singing style, the Irish composer Seán Ó Riada said:

> In approaching that style of singing which is called in Irish, the Sean Nós – the old style –
> it is best to listen as if we were listening to music for the first time, with a child's new mind;
> or to think of Indian music rather than European.[1]

Sean Nós singing is solo, unaccompanied singing, a characteristic that it shares with the European ballad style. However, Sean Nós singing never developed along the lines of ballad singing which came to incorporate harmony, group singing and accompaniment. Sean Nós remains oral in its method of transmission, so it is a very pure, old, primitive form of singing. It is also a challenging and complex form to master, and requires that the singer have or acquire Irish language competency. Its best performers are rightly acclaimed as artists of unsurpassed excellence.

This is perhaps the most distinctive of Irish musical forms. Where the Irish language did not survive, the style died out. Nor, unlike the resilient instrumental music, did it survive beyond one generation in America. It is easy to see why the Sean Nós song and the singer who breathes life into it carry such a precious cultural message. Sean Nós involves the transmission of the pure spirit of an ancient and timeless cultural message. The acclaimed traditional musician, Tony MacMahon, speaks of the "intensely lyrical line" of Sean Nós singing and is of the opinion that "traditional singing in the Irish language is at the centre of our music".

Songs in English

The process of British colonisation in Ireland went hand in hand with the demise of Irish as the spoken language of the people.

According to Breandán Breathnach, so few Irish songs made a successful transition into English that "one may deduce a rule that folk songs do not pass from one language to another".[2]

In musical terms, the changeover from Irish to English meant adopting the English ballad. By the word "ballad" is meant a narrative song or poem, although again there are problems of definition

---

[1] Seán Ó Riada, *Our Musical Heritage* (Funduireacht an Riadaigh, 1982), p. 23.
[2] Breandán Breathnach, *Folk Music and Dances of Ireland* (Mercier Press, Cork, 1971).

and songs that fall outside this category, e.g. nonsense songs, lullabies, work songs, carols, etc. There are straightforward "imports" from England to Ireland – songs like "Barbara Allen" and "Little Musgrave".

But folk songs did not die with the demise of Irish and there also began a tradition of new songs composed in the new language, English. Often these new songs were written to fit existing airs borrowed from many sources: English, Scottish, or Irish. This is a practice that has continued to the present day, as anyone familiar with the songs of Bob Dylan, for example, will know.

Not every singer made so free and easy with Irish airs, though. The nineteenth-century Irish writer William Carelton tells in his autobiography that his mother, a fine singer, did not like to sing English songs to Irish airs. When requested to sing such a song, she replied: "I'll sing it for you, but the English words and the air are like quarrelling man and wife; the Irish melts into the tune, but the English doesn't."

Very often these songs in English were printed as "broadsheets" to be sold in the streets by itinerant ballad singers, travelling singers and travelling people who also sang at fairs, races and other events. There were local songs, old songs, and new songs printed on the broadsheets which, by all accounts, enjoyed a brisk trade. People bought the broadsheet to learn the song and thus it passed into the folk song repertoire. Sometimes these songs endured for a very long time and became classics; sometimes they perished and were forgotten, like the ephemeral pop songs of today.

Classical Music

Ireland has no classical music tradition in the European art-music sense. As the Irish classically trained composer Seán Ó Riada pointed out, Ireland has a highly developed and complex music which, just because it was orally transmitted, should not be considered solely as folk music. He often made the parallel between this kind of music and the equally highly developed music of oriental cultures, also orally transmitted.

Into these "classical" categories can be admitted Sean Nós singing, hailed by Irish musicologist and composer Seoirse Bodley as:

> one of the greatest achievements of the Irish people in traditional music and [which] is also superbly complex music in its own right. Using the simplest of means, voice alone, it can demand of the singer the greatest artistry.

The other category is the instrumental music of the old Irish harping tradition, which was the music of the Irish aristocracy, both native Irish and those descended from the first Anglo-Norman colonisation of Ireland. This latter class had become so intermarried with the native Irish that, in a much-vaunted historical cliché, they became "more Irish than the Irish themselves".

This absorption of Irish culture involved the patronage of harpers, who were the equivalent of court musicians. It is recorded that Queen Elizabeth I had an Irish harper at her court by the name of Dónal Buidhe.

The harp itself figured as an instrument of importance in ancient Irish legend. There is documentary evidence of its existence in Ireland from the eighth century. There was also a standard Irish harp of distinctive make and style with its own repertoire.

The harpers composed for their patrons special pieces of music, of sophisticated and complex construction. Sadly, most of this music is lost to us. We do know that the harps were metal strung and that the harper played with his nails grown long for the purpose. The sound quality obviously was nothing like that achieved by the gut and nylon-strung "Irish" harps of today, which the modern harpist plays with the flesh of the fingers (for more about the harp and its music, see Chapter Eight).

In a way, this tradition contained the seeds of its own destruction, dependent as it was for its existence on a class whose days were numbered if complete colonisation was to be achieved. The realisation of that objective meant dispossession or surrender.

To go "downmarket" and become a folk musician was not really an option. The music of the harpers was incomprehensible to those outside the old order. It faded away and with it went at least a thousand years of a great tradition.

The Spirit of the Music

The idea of journey is a recurring theme in the history of Irish music and with this idea of journey goes its expressed perception of exile. This is especially true of the music. Why leaving the home place should be invariably conceived of as exile, even when it presaged an improvement in life, is bound up with the pre-eminence of landscape in Irish minds and hearts.

There is even a word in Irish for it: "dinnseanchas", meaning literally the lore of place names, but referring also to the ancient practice of writing poems and songs in praise of places. The Irish poet Seamus Heaney is a contemporary "dinnseanchas" poet for whom this cast in the Irish mind marks Ireland out as more than a geographical country but a "country of the mind". This country of the mind is embedded in the sound and texture of traditional music, even in the names of the tunes themselves: "The Humours of Carrigaholt", "The Walls of Limerick", "The Rocky Road to Dublin", "The Glen Road to Carrick", "The Boys of Bluehill", and so on. They present a map of the musical landscape townland by townland, village by village, and field by field.

It is easier to leave the geographical country than the interior landscape, and many Irish "exiles" never did. Heaney says: "This love of place and lamentation against exile from a cherished territory is another typical strain in the Celtic sensibility."[3] This image of exile can also operate as

---

[3] Seamus Heaney, "The God in the Tree, Early Irish Nature Poetry" in *Preoccupations – Selected Prose 1968–1978* (Faber & Faber, 1984).

perceived internal exile. The feeling that, for historical reasons, the Irish person is a stranger in his own land and the longing to "come back" is often articulated in music.

Preoccupation with and love for landscape, feelings of loneliness, and the force of memory came through again and again in the making of *Bringing It All Back Home* amongst musicians in Ireland, England, and America, not only in the area of traditional music. Tony MacMahon, the accordion player from County Clare, spoke eloquently of:

> The old feelings; the belief that rocks and rivers and mountains are inhabited by spirits – they're not just shapes – they're three dimensional beings . . . and I think that that tune ['Port na bPúcaí, a slow air] is a lonely way of bringing that out, which is the reason I like to play it.

Máire Ní Bhraonáin, of the group Clannad, said:

> You know that when we've made an album . . . the judgment day for me is when I'm going home to Donegal and . . . I put the cassette on then, and if I feel it's worthy of the area, then I'm happy with it . . . so that's how I judge my music . . . I love going home to Donegal; it is definitely the sole inspiration of Clannad in the long run.

Kentucky-born country musician Ricky Skaggs echoed these sentiments:

> I feel the Irish tunes had a happy lilt . . . and those tunes were brought over to America years and years ago and it seems as if those first or second generation children that grew up playing those tunes started missing their homeland and missing their folks. There was a sadness and a pining and a lonesomeness that just seemed to enter the music, and you know when your heart's broken . . . you're gonna play from your heart, you're gonna play much more lonesome feelings and to me that's where that Appalachian Mountain, that High Lonesome Sound . . . came into being.

Two

That High Lonesome Sound

But the rents were getting higher
And we could no longer stay,
So farewell unto you
Bonny, bonny, Slieve Gallion Braes.

These are the last lines of the song "Slieve Gallion Braes", sung for *Bringing It All Back Home* by Dolores Keane with John Faulkener and sister Christine. Slieve Gallion is a mountain in County Tyrone in the north of Ireland, an area which became, after the partition of the country in 1921, part of the state of Northern Ireland. It is a place of great beauty, lovingly described in the song:

As I went a-roaming one morning in May
To view the fair valleys and mountains so gay
I was thinking of the flowers all doomed to decay
That bloom around ye bonny, bonny Slieve Gallion Braes.

The story behind the song is that of the overwhelming emigration from that part of Ireland in the eighteenth century. The inhabitants of the area, mostly small farmers, were Presbyterians of Scottish stock and relatively recently arrived. Most of them had settled in this province of Ireland during the so-called Ulster Plantation of the seventeenth century.

In some respects they resembled the older Catholic native Irish, having come from the same kind of agricultural economy with similar traditions. Like the native Irish they suffered religious persecution. In the eighteenth century this, economic distress caused by bad harvests, and high rents combined to push them out. These people made up the first mass Irish migration to America. Their going had impacted on the song-making in Ireland long after they had been absorbed into American society. A huge store of Irish emigration songs date from this time. These emigrants settled in the Appalachian mountain regions of east-coast America. They were known as the Scots-Irish and the music and songs they brought with them were subsumed into American folk music. The aspects of culture which they brought with them underwent a transformation over time and became Appalachian old-time music, song and dance.

This Appalachian sound would go on to play a role in the making of a quintessential American musical style: rock 'n' roll.

Exodus

The rents were getting higher
and we could no longer stay

High rents and an unjust and repressive landlord-tenant system existed in eighteenth-century Ulster.

It's not for the want of employment at home,
That caused all the sons of old Ireland to roam,
But those tyrannising landlords,
They would not let us stay
So farewell unto ye
Bonny, bonny Slieve Gallion Braes.

The system of land-owning in Ireland was characterised by a high degree of absenteeism; one third or more of landowners lived in Britain and saw their estates and hapless tenants as a source of income and nothing else. They preferred to make money by increasing rents and very few invested in improvements. By 1711 the average annual rent of an acre of Irish land was equivalent to the purchase price of an acre of land in America. Once people became aware of better conditions abroad they were provided with a powerful incentive to leave. The sentiments of many emigrants of this time are expressed in another Ulster song, "The Rambling Irishman":

But to live poor, I could not endure,
Like others of my station,
To Amerikay I sailed away,
And left this Irish nation.

Whole congregations and communities moved *en masse* to escape religious persecution. America was seen as a country where the liberty to worship in freedom would be guaranteed, and where the means to support a decent standard of living could be maintained. This mass movement often took the form of a pastor leading his whole flock out to the new country, taking with them farm implements, seeds for planting – and their singing tradition and music.

It is chilling to imagine the social disruption caused as the homesteads of whole parishes were sold up and deserted. It is not surprising that songs of emigration which recount the events of that time are still sung. For most of the eighteenth century, seventy-five per cent of Irish emigrants were

Protestants; nearly three quarters of these were Presbyterians. The rest were Anglicans, Quakers and of other Protestant denominations.

From a country in which the overwhelming population was Catholic, this represented an enormous number of people. Somewhere between 200,000 and 300,000 Protestants emigrated during the first seventy-five years of the eighteenth century.

Davy Hammond is a Belfast man, a singer and a film-maker. He has made many programmes about the music and song culture of Northern Ireland. Hammond makes the point forcibly that these early Presbyterian emigrants, like their Catholic neighbours, were aesthetically involved with their landscape and "mourned very grievously for the place they left, and these emigration songs are always about that . . . about leaving the hills and the fields and the small streams". For them "the landscape was very informative. It charged their emotional life and their imagination".

America – Land of Liberty

It is true to say that there was no homogeneous Protestant migration. Some emigrants were well-to-do and certainly not leaving under compulsion of poverty or persecution. Neither was the migration uniformly rural. There were both tradesmen and town dwellers. Nevertheless, most of those who left were from rural backgrounds, small-holdings at that. Some of them were forced by poverty to offer themselves as indentured servants in return for the passage money. This was *de facto* slavery. Indentureship was a system whereby the person wishing to emigrate signed himself over, usually, to the shipmaster for a stipulated term. The shipmaster then sold his services as a servant on the other side. Another way was to sign on with a better-off farmer who needed farm workers in America and become his indentured servant. The ultimate goal was to serve the time, finish the indenture, and then buy some land. Land ownership would have been beyond the means of rack-rent paying tenantry in Ulster.

Emigrants' aspirations were traditional. Ambition and self-interest had not yet been made virtues. America was seen as a place where there was ample land, no landlord, no rent, and where a family could be supported in comfort.

The pattern of settlement of this migration was diverse, spread as it was over a wide area of America and including cities and towns. The particular settlement that is of interest in the story of *Bringing It All Back Home* is that of the Appalachian Scots or Scots-Irish. In the Appalachian mountain country of Virginia, West Virginia, Kentucky, Tennessee, North and South Carolina, Irish music evolved into what has become known as "That High Lonesome Sound".

The singing tradition brought by the Scots-Irish was English language balladry for the most part. This would have meant unaccompanied solo singing at the time. Some of the ballads would have come from Scotland and England. There would also have been songs of more recent local composition. According to the late song collector, Seán O'Baoill:

Immigrants awaiting processing at Ellis Island, New York, in 1910.

[T]he two main tributaries, Scots and English, flow into the main Irish stream of Ulster folk song. Ever since the Battle of Kinsale in 1601, there has been a constant interchange of songs between Ireland and Britain.[2]

For reasons of expediency and taste, English and Scots ballads were adapted to Irish airs and Irish language idioms found their way into new ballads in English. There were songs in Irish in abundance, but with the decline of the language in Ulster many of these songs and some of the airs disappeared. It is not always possible at this remove to be specific about the origins of individual songs because, as O'Baoill said, "the traditions so overlap and intertwine that it's impossible to dogmatise about the origins of some songs either in words or in music".[3]

---

[2] Seán O'Baoill, "Traditional Singing in English – The Ulster Dimension", *Treoir* (February, 1974), p. 8.
[3] *Ibid.*

Certainly there was and is a distinct singing tradition in Ulster. Davy Hammond identifies this style as one where "the music would run to a more rhythmic line, [and] you wouldn't have the same number of grace notes or decorations [as in the rest of Ireland]". That this tradition travelled with emigrants to America is not in doubt. In some cases, the songs even remained exactly the same as when they left.

O'Baoill instanced the example of the Scots ballad "The Knight on the Road", which he recorded from a traditional singer in County Tyrone in the fifties. The melody was an air known as "The Uist Tramping Song". Before this, two living versions of the song had been recorded: one, unsurprisingly, in the Highlands of Scotland; the other in the Appalachian mountains in the thirties. He reckoned that it had been known in Ulster for over two hundred years. The Ulster or Scots-Irish element in Appalachia was well established by the end of the eighteenth century. Historian Kerby Miller estimated that "50% or more of the settlers on the trans-Appalachian frontier were of Ulster lineage".[4] Here they met other settlers of English, Swedish and German extraction. Over generations they intermarried and founded communities, until eventually it became impossible to identify an "Ulster American" community as such.

The American ethnomusicologist Alan Lomax wrote of the musical interaction of these early settlers:

> The Southern mountains preserved the traditional ballads, lyric songs, and dance tunes in comparative isolation, thus permitting the emergence of hybrid songs, which were on the one hand fusions of Scots, Irish and English influences and on the other genuine reflections of pioneer culture patterns.[5]

"As I Roved Out . . . Old King Cole" in County Armagh

Jean Ritchie is a traditional singer from Viper, in Perry County, south-eastern Kentucky, now living in Long Island, New York. She comes from a long line of singers of "mountain music" and has written a wonderful account of those early days at home with her family in *Singing Family of The Cumberlands*. Ritchie has a huge store of songs which were:

> handed down from the old people. They came from Scotland, England and Ireland, Wales maybe. My father's name was Ritchie and my mother's name was Hall . . . she was English and he was Scottish, and there were a lot of Irish, Welsh, and a few German families, and we all got intermarried so that the music got sort of intermarried too . . . so in Kentucky there's a great melting pot of all those countries' music.

---

[4] Kerby Miller, *Emigrants and Exiles – Ireland and the Irish Exodus to North America* (OUP, 1985), p. 161.
[5] John and Alan Lomax, *Best Loved American Folk Songs* (Grosset and Dunlop, 1947), Preface.

Ritchie was born in 1922, the last of fourteen children. Her elder brothers and sisters remembered a time before the advent of the railroad when "there weren't even any instruments – we didn't even have a dulcimer . . . in the old days they just sang, they didn't have any accompaniment to their voice". This style of singing would have been much the same as traditional singing in Ireland and Britain, melodic and unaccompanied. Unlike the mainstream mother tradition, there was some unison singing.

The scarcity of instruments had come about partly because of faith-based anathema (they were deemed "instruments of the devil"), poverty, and non-availability. However, the dance tunes did not die out either. They became incorporated into "play songs":

> When you danced and you didn't have a fiddle . . . you made the rhythm with your hands and you just sang the song, and the people who weren't dancing would stand on the side and help sing and help do the rhythm.

There were old ballads like "Barbara Allen" and lullabies, and "just any kind of song you can think of".

Later on came big changes: the railroad in 1911, then coal mining, the first music recordings, and finally the radio. All these were to influence a way of life that had gone on more or less undisturbed for two hundred years. It was to affect the music in many ways, too.

In 1952 Ritchie received a Fulbright scholarship to research the origins of some of her family's music in the British Isles. With her went her husband George Pickow, who served as photographer and sound recordist for the expedition. Initially Ritchie planned to visit England, Scotland and Wales only. When she told her English supervisor, a professor at London University, that folk music was the subject of her research, he told her that she must go to Ireland. And so, "we started in Ireland and we spent a long time there, longer than in any other country, because we fell in love with the people and with the music".

She did not have long to wait before she made a connection with her musical "roots". It happened in the kitchen of Sara Makem, a traditional singer who lived in the little town of Keady, County Armagh.

> I have a wonderful recording of her getting supper or tea for us while she's singing and talking to us . . . she's singing, you can hear the knife go through the bread – rar! rar! rar! – and you can hear the bacon sizzling. All the time she's singing "As I roved out on a May morning, on a May morning right early".

> I kept listening to it and smelling the bacon and being reminded of something . . . it was a play game that we played back home; it was called "Old King Cole was a Jolly Old Soul" and it used almost the same tune as she was using. So that's how the music got there! Sometimes the words were changed but the tune remained the same. They had a way of keeping the Irish tunes mostly because Irish tunes were far superior, of course!

Her journey was full of such discoveries, but this one she cherishes dearly:

Traditional singer Elizabeth Cronin talks with Jean Ritchie (right) in County Cork, 1952.

She sings her little song and it's so pretty, and it's one of my most treasured recordings; it's nothing you could ever put on a record or anything but I listen to it and I'm reminded of that lovely day.

The song "As I Roved Out", as it happened, was very well known to listeners to a folk music programme of the same name on BBC radio in the late forties and fifties. A fragment of the song sung by Sara was the signature tune.

Sara's son, Tommy Makem, who began his musical career with the Clancy Brothers, told a touching story about this same tune and its effect on a man from his and Sara's home town of Keady. This man was

> away in Africa somewhere . . . and he had broken his leg or something; he was in hospital, anyway, and he was feeling very sad for himself . . . He turned on his radio on Sunday morning [to the BBC World Service] and there was Sara Makem singing. He told me (and he was a big strong man) that he broke down and cried because it brought something of home to him.

From Coleraine, County Derry, to Mulenberg County, Kentucky

In 1811 the Irish collector Edward Bunting noted down a song called "Rose Connolly" from a singer in Coleraine, County Derry, in Northern Ireland. He also noted that the author and the date were unknown. He published the song tune in his 1840 collection, *The Ancient Music of Ireland*; and this is the extent of the information known about "Rose(y) Connolly" in Ireland, except for a text of the song taken down in 1929 by a collector from a singer in County Galway. The words identify the song as a murder ballad. The unfortunate Rose(y) is killed by her lover. Although no reason is given, the subtext is probably that of a pregnant girl deserted by her lover.

The late American scholar D.K. Wilgus, who researched the origins of "Rose Connolly", outlined the connection between it and a more famous Irish song called "Down by the Salley Gardens". The words of the song were written by the Irish poet W.B. Yeats. He adapted the lyrics from a song he had heard sung in his youth by an elderly woman in County Sligo.

> *Down by the salley gardens my love and I did meet.*

A willow tree in Ireland is also known as a salley tree. The other name by which "Rose Connolly" is known in America is "Down in the Willow Garden":

> *Down in a Willow Garden*
> *Where me and my love did meet*

All Phil Everly of the Everly Brothers knew about the song was that "it always just seemed to be there . . . the song was one of those traditional songs that people would sing", while his brother Don commented: "Our father had a big song book and he had the lyrics to hundreds and hundreds of songs and he knew them all and, you know, we were never smart enough to ask him where he found them." On this, as on previous occasions, when they have performed "Rose Connolly", the Everlys like to be accompanied by Irish uilleann pipe player Liam O'Flynn, whom they first met in Ireland some years ago.

Although they never thought about it much, there was an unconscious assumption on their part that the origin of much of the music which they played was Irish, Scottish or English.

I think you can really see the influence of Irish music in the harmonics, at least in the harmony singing . . . there [are] a lot of fifths and what I call "spreads" in Irish fiddle playing and you can hear that, and in the pipes too, you can hear those spreads.

They were disappointed to find no trace of an Irish Everly on their first trip there in the fifties:

Everyone sort of assumed we were Irish anyway . . . but the name Everly is not in Ireland . . . we had heard that the name was O'Everly, like "Of Everly", and when we got to Ireland they said, "Well, sorry" . . . We tried very hard to be Irish.

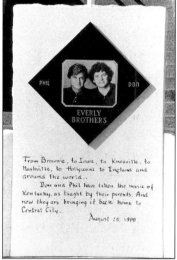

The Everlys' family background is Mulenberg County, Kentucky, although they spent most of their youth in Shenendoah, Iowa. Their father, like the rest of the community in Mulenberg County, had begun his working life at a young age in the coal mine, which he quit, ending up as a professional musician in a Chicago nightclub. He eventually moved to Iowa where he had his own radio show on which Don and Phil joined him as soon as they were able to sing.

Unlike Jean Ritchie, who grew up singing as part of a family tradition to provide their own entertainment, the Everlys were part of the new phenomenon of radio. Don and Phil had the unusual experience as children of going to the radio station every morning before school to sing on a live show. They did maintain contact with their Kentucky roots and still do. As children they would sing on the porch with the family as Jean Ritchie did. In addition to songs like "Down in the Willow Garden" they would sing songs popularised on the radio "'cause we were trying to be,

Plaque in honour of the Everly Brothers in their home town of Central City, Kentucky.

you know, Hank Williams and Lefty Frizell and whatever else we could hear". They went on from those porch try-outs to become stars in their own right and recorded a string of hits in the sixties. They combined the country harmonies they had learned as children with a contemporary rhythmic base to produce the unique Everly Brothers sound.

This comes through on the old folk song "Down in the Willow Garden" as much as it does on the waltz-time "Darling don't let our Love Die" (a hit for a thirties singing group) which was also recorded during the *Bringing It All Back Home* session in Nashville.

The Everly Brothers.

Radio, Railroads and Coal Mines

It would be difficult to underestimate the impact radio had on those communities in the Appalachians and on their music. Before the radio arrived, music was local. Many of the communities were isolated and inaccessible. The radio had been preceded by the first commercial recordings and the arrival of the record-player – the "Victrola" or "talkin' machine", as it was referred to in Jean Ritchie's youth.

Ritchie recalls her father ordering a Victrola from a mail-order catalogue and travelling a couple of days' journey with a sled and mule to collect it from the depot. It was an object of wonder and amazement wherever he played it. This was the first such machine in Viper.

The radio which followed soon after had an even more profound impact on music-making in the community. What was happening was "the transformation of Southern white music from its 'folk' (or non-commercial) origins into the music associated with the term 'hillbilly'".[6] Traditional music was beginning to detach itself from its host culture and that culture itself was being changed in the process.

Initially the difference was not in the tunes or songs themselves; it was in the way they were played and sung. Gradually the emphasis shifted, from one or two instrumental performers playing together, to bands. Groups of musicians and singers played with mandolins, guitars, autoharps, fiddles and banjos backing them. The music was catchy and included harmonies and backing arrangements hitherto unheard in traditional music and song. For Abigail Ritchie, Jean's mother, the radio was a vehicle for "pure devil music . . . all these instruments and this rhythm".

> Prior to radio and phonograph recordings, songs and dances were performed unselfcon-sciously. There was little concern for arrangement, aesthetic production, or tonal balance, and practically no concern at all about the total length of a performance.[7]

The radio changed all this. The musical life of America was never the same again. In Appalachia it created the professional "folk" musician.

Professional musicians were not unknown. They worked in vaudeville and in travelling shows. But country people in Appalachia, as in rural Ireland, had been musically self-sufficient in Jean Ritchie's youth. Radio was now replacing the home entertainers. Because of radio, a musician like Ike Everly was given an alternative to working all his life in a coal mine: "Dad played guitar and that guitar got him to Chicago, and of course . . . we had a better chance at life," said Phil Everly. Coal mining, following hard on the railroad, presaged another disruption in Kentucky. Initially it meant steady work and a better living than subsistence farming could provide. Ultimately it spelled disaster for the fragile ecology of the mountains: polluted rivers and stripped land, worked-out mines and economic collapse.

---

[6] Earl V. Spielman, *Traditional North American Fiddling* (PhD thesis, University of Wisconsin, Madison, 1975), p. 244.
[7] *Ibid.*, p. 246.

Jean Ritchie recording piper Seamus Ennis in Ireland, 1952.

Jean Ritchie has written many songs about the impact of the coal mine on Kentucky. Some of these songs have travelled around the world and entered the repertoire of contemporary folk singers. "The L and N Don't Stop Here Anymore" is a song she wrote about a railway line that fell into disuse when the coal ran out. It has been recorded by singer-songwriter Michelle Shocked and by country singer Johnny Cash. More recently, Irish singer-songwriter Tony Small learned the song from an English folk singer in Germany, unaware of its provenance or of any of these recordings – it had become part of a network of oral transmission.

In this way commercial recordings or learned versions of them renew the store of contemporary folk songs. True folk song can be depended upon to be recognised for what it is. As Elmer

Bernstein put it: "I think you can tell what's a real folk song and what's a phoney, because the real ones do have the soul of the people in them."

"Paradise" is a song written by John Prine about the devastation wrought by strip-mining in Kentucky. He recorded it for *Bringing It All Back Home* at the Nashville sessions. Prine shares family roots in Mulenberg County with the Everlys. Like Don and Phil's father, Prine's parents headed for Chicago to work and rear their family. They, too, returned regularly to the old hometown, the unfortunately-named Paradise. To clear the way for strip-mining, the entire town of Paradise was demolished. Today the area has changed beyond all recognition: "Actually," says Don Everly, "if I remember correctly you used to drive uphill to Mulenberg from Nashville – now you drive kind of down."

The Depression of the thirties forced many rural people from the Appalachians and other parts of the south to move out, to cities or other areas. By doing so they extended the audience for country music. Although the recording industry was in decline for much of the thirties, radio expanded and networked radio broadcast country music nationwide.

> Network radio sought to reach and develop a national audience, and therefore attempted
> to reduce many of the local and regional differences. In music especially, radio contributed
> to a homogeneity of styles.[8]

All music was grist to radio's mill. On radio many musical influences came together – jazz, blues, ragtime, cowboy songs, Cajun, mariachi, in combination with white Anglo-Saxon traditional music. The result of this interaction was to be seen in the string bands and singing groups, in the bluegrass, Texas swing and singing cowboys of the next two decades.

---

[8] *Ibid.*, p. 255.

All looked to the traditional source for tunes and sounds. They mixed them with outside musical influences, producing new songs and material with which their particular band or group was then identified. Radio created a near-insatiable demand for material. The entire traditional repertoire was used to supply the demand, as was every other musical form available. Later on, rock 'n' roll, electrification of instruments, and pop had a levelling effect on these hybrids. In an attempt to sound "poppy" and "rocky" much country music became bland and featureless by adopting the worst characteristics of formula pop and rock. Much of what came to be regarded as the "Nashville sound" fitted into this category and its influence spread beyond Nashville. Fortunately, what rock 'n' roll and pop did was not all bad news for country music. Rock 'n' roll was, after all, born in the south.

Some of this "hillbilly" or "old-time" music of the early radio days took root in odd corners of the world, including Ireland. The Lee Valley String Band in Cork in the south of Ireland is a case in point. They play a mixture of traditional and old-time material in the style of the singing and instrumental groups of the twenties and thirties. The instrumental line-up is fiddle, banjo, mandolin, autoharp, and guitar. Songs come from sources like the Carter family and Bill Monroe. Matt Cranitch, a traditional musician and former fiddle player with the Lee Valley, met a fiddler from Nashville passing through Cork, who provided him with an introduction to the music of the Appalachians. It was a mutually fruitful meeting: "He asked me to show him a few reels and I said, 'I will if you show me a few tunes', and I did, and he did, and here I am playing with these lads."

Sharon Shannon is one of the best known and most innovative of the younger generation of accordion players. Although rooted in the distinctive traditional music of her native County Clare and an accomplished player in this style, she works across many traditionally based genres. At one musical intersection she encountered the country musician Steve Earle. Out of the experience came the wonderful "Galway Girl", a song written by Earle and recorded by both musicians and included on each of the albums released by the artists in 2000.

Three

The Stranger's Land

Sorrow filled me leaving Ireland
when I was powerful,
so that mournful grief came to me
in the foreign land

When emigration began to feature as a fact of life for Irish people, the Irish psyche was disposed to internalise it as exile. The Irish emigrant departed in circumstances of famine in the mid-nineteenth century, and rural poverty or stagnation in later years. This, coupled with the colonial status of Ireland, added to the sense of enforced exile. It is reflected in a tradition of emigration songs which is now three hundred years old and which has its roots in the earliest poetry of Gaelic Ireland.

The theme of enforced exile from the much-loved home place accompanied by an almost pagan celebration of nature are enduring threads through Irish poetry and song. A monastic poet of the twelfth century put the words shown above in the mouth of the sixth-century saint, Colum Cille (founder of the city of Derry in Northern Ireland). The poem goes on to praise the places the saint loves, displays a great joy in nature, and finishes on a note of bitter regret and longing for home:

> I have loved the lands of Ireland, I speak truth; it would be delightful to spend the night with Comgall and visit Canice.[1]

The sentiments expressed in this twelfth-century poem would have struck the hearts of Irish listeners down through the centuries. The beauty of the poem, its unsentimental yet emotional expressiveness, is also characteristic of a particular genre of Irish songs of exile.

Successive centuries of invasion and colonisation – Viking, Norman, and English – brought about consciousness of an internal exile. Many Irish saw themselves as "strangers in their own land", dispossessed and suffering under the tyranny of foreigners.

---

[1] Colum Cille, *A Golden Treasury of Irish Poetry* (David Greene and Frank O'Connor Eds, Macmillan, London, 1967).

Feelings of exile and dispossession were not universal. They were dependent, to some degree, on time and place. Where colonisation was successful and where English became the spoken language of the native Irish, the old ways were displaced. As the Irish poet Thomas Kinsella said: "The loss was not regretted in English-speaking Ireland, in so far as it was felt at all."[2]

Irish Emigration before the Famine

The first Catholic Irish emigrants to reach America were not, as is often supposed, victims of the famine of the 1840s. For a full century and longer they had been coming to America as transported convicts and indentured servants, sometimes kidnapped for the purpose, so high was the demand for labour in the colonies. They met prejudice and ill-treatment. Many, unable to withstand the climatic conditions, died of tropical diseases. It was soon realised that black slave labour was more suited to the purpose and the experiment in white Irish slave trading did not last.

Otherwise, Irish Catholic emigrants tended to be either adventurer members of the lower gentry, artisans or itinerant labourers. The majority were males travelling alone. They tended to disappear into the American hinterland without establishing themselves in any kind of ethnically focused Irish community.

The nineteenth century in Ireland saw many changes. The first and most obvious one was the explosion in population growth from four million in 1780 to seven million in 1821. There was also an increase in the use of English and in literacy in that language. Communications and transport improved and restrictions on travel out of the country were lifted. The pace of emigration picked up and Catholics began to outnumber Protestant emigrants. The so-called "American letters" began to arrive. These were letters sent home by emigrants to relatives usually containing money. Indeed, the "American letter" was a synonym for money. If the letter did not contain any, no-one would advertise the fact. The letter more often than not contained the passage money for the next-in-line member of the family to travel out.

In 1838 fifty per cent of Irish emigrants' fares were paid by family members already living in America. Initially, the popular route was by sea from Liverpool to New York, the fare costing between two and three pounds. From the mid-1820s poorer people began to make up the numbers of those emigrating, numbers which increased or were maintained at a high level from then on.

Emigration to Britain in this period also increased and, indeed, was preferred by poorer Irish people who could not afford the fare to America. The fare for a channel crossing was ten pence or less. Two hundred thousand Irish people left for Britain between 1830 and 1835. The ranks of Irish emigrants in Liverpool were swelled by those who had set out for the first leg of the journey to America. Having been fleeced of all their money by unscrupulous ticket-brokers and innkeepers, they were forced

---

2   Thomas Kinsella, *New Oxford Book of Irish Verse* (OUP, 1986), Introduction, p. xxv.

to stay in Liverpool. These Irish immigrants, destitute and unskilled, found themselves at the bottom of the social ladder in English cities, living in slums, employed (if at all) in lowly paid occupations.

By now there was also a long-established pattern of seasonal migration from the north and west of Ireland to Scotland, and from the south and east of Ireland to London and the English Midlands. These migrants would have included families travelling together to work in the textile industry, or men looking for work as navvies.

The Ireland they were leaving behind was one in which it was becoming harder to maintain even a subsistence standard of living. Fierce competition for land was forcing rents up to unaffordable levels. Smallholders could not afford improvements like drainage or fertiliser, so their land was inefficiently used. The practice of dividing up a family holding into smaller and smaller plots between members was putting intolerable pressure on the land to produce enough to keep families fed.

The potato was a crop which yielded well and was nutritious. Supplemented by buttermilk, eggs, or fowl, it provided a fairly healthy diet. By the late 1840s the struggle to pay rent had engulfed smallholders, cottiers, and landless labourers. Seventy-five per cent of the rural population of Ireland was totally dependent on the potato as the sole source of food. When potato stocks ran low before the

THE IRISH FAMINE: SCENE AT THE GATE OF A WORKHOUSE.

An etching of distress caused by the Potato Famine – peasants clamouring for admission to the Kinross Union workhouse, hoping for something to eat, 1847.

harvest, destitution and near-starvation were commonplace. In spite of this, music-making was still an activity that was widely enjoyed and highly valued. Mícheál Ó Súilleabháin described the circumstances:

> You had this situation of poverty and perhaps because of that there was a lot more leisure time; so it's ironic that leisure time can come out of having too much money and can also come out of having not enough. And all we know is that what we call Irish traditional music, the Sean Nós singing, the dance music tradition and the dancing itself, is the product of these people.

The Great Famine

Between 1845 and 1855 the face of Ireland was changed forever. In those ten years one million people died from famine and disease. As Peadar Ó Riada observed:

> You'd a population of some eight and a half million people, and between famine, and emigration and . . . disease and everything else, it was decimated down to two and a half million. Now in the space of eighty years, if you do that even to a herd of elephants . . . you're going to cause havoc . . . and the Irish nation, and the Irish people as a whole have a huge psychic hurt which they have pushed way down to the subconscious, but it's still there, and it comes out in various forms.

The issue of the Famine has generated a continuing controversy in Ireland in recent years, both amongst scholars and the general population. There is evidence that, as Peadar Ó Riada said, the enormity of what happened has been too painful to confront. In 1845 a new strain of blight struck about thirty per cent of the potato crop and destroyed it; in 1846 it destroyed almost all of the crop; and for every year after that until the mid-fifties, to a greater or lesser degree, the crop failed. With such a large section of the population totally dependent on the potato, the failure of the crop brought complete devastation. There were scenes of death and disease on a scale never before recorded in Irish history. People wandered about the country scavenging for food, dying in the streets, or waiting for death in their cabins. In her autobiography, Peig Sayers, an inhabitant of Great Blasket Island off the Kerry coast, recalls her father's account of the Great Famine or "The Bad Times":

> "Sixteen years of age I was, Muiris," he said, "when my uncle died with the hunger . . . whatever bit of food was going he preferred to give it to the family so as to keep them alive, but God help us, he failed! The world was too hard . . . Hunger got the upper hand of him and he died."[3]

---

[3] Sayers, *The Autobiography of Peig Sayers of the Great Blasket Island* (trans. Bryan MacMahon, Talbot Press, 1974).

Attempts at relief proved inadequate or came too late. Local areas were left to cope with the crisis as best they might. In the west, which was worse affected, the fragile structure of public relief collapsed under the strain. Voluntary agencies like the Quakers, money from America, and some landlords stemmed the tide here and there, but these efforts were not equal to relieving the distress.

Over two million people left the country, including family groups with young children and infirm, elderly people. In the wake of those fleeing went artisans and tradesmen whose means of earning a living now had collapsed.

For the first time large numbers left the Irish-speaking areas in the west, which had been very badly hit. In all, perhaps 350,000 Irish speakers emigrated. They were even less well equipped to deal with emigration than those for whom English was their mother tongue. Irish speakers, handicapped by their lack of English, had few resources with which to deal with the world to which they were going. Their experience of dislocation was intensified on this account.

Those who left and those who died were among the most vulnerable – the landless labourers and the smallholders who had no other means of subsistence or way of earning a living outside agriculture.

As if to underline the agony, exports of Irish grain continued uninterrupted throughout the famine years, as did rent incomes to absentee landlords in England. This was remembered with bitterness by those who survived the famine. A man by the name of Madigan, of Kilrush, County Clare, composed a song in the 1850s or 1860s which deals with the connected issues of famine and emigration. He did not regard the famine as an "Act of God". The fact was that, in addition to British misman-agement, wilful ignorance and callousness, there was a section of Irish Catholic farmers who actually did well out of the famine. They used the disaster to rid themselves of unproductive tenants and consolidate their holdings. These tenants were evicted and left to fend for themselves. When Peig Sayers' father reminisced about famine times, his friend Muiris replied: "Hey, man! . . . Isn't that how the big farmers came by all the land they have today!"[4]

The Catholic clergy hampered the relief work of Protestant charities. They feared some of their flock might "turn", i.e. convert to Protestantism, if they accepted the soup being offered by these charities. This was considered to be a greater danger than death from starvation. Even today in Ireland the expression "to take the soup" connotes a sell-out or betrayal.

These subtleties were buried in the upsurge of nationalist feelings in the years that followed the famine. The guilt that survival imposed on those who made it through the catastrophe was also a factor in the after effects and it has taken generations for the shock waves to recede. Survival could engender shame from a sense that this was achieved at the expense of others weaker and more vulnerable. It's not surprising, then, that England became the focus of the anger and the "psychic hurt" Peadar Ó Riada spoke of. The spirits of the "coffinless graves of Poor Erin" would have to be appeased.

---

[4] *Ibid.*, p. 62.

Interestingly, there is little in the song culture that relates to events which took place during that terrible episode in Irish history. One that is well known and is a "big song" in the Sean Nós tradition is "Johnny Seoighe" (Johnny Joyce), set in Connemara during the Famine. "Johnny Seoighe" challenges the singer to inhabit the emotional landscape of this most desolate of songs with its dominant theme of despair.

The New Island

Aftershocks from the famine were felt for many years. Reorganisation of agriculture begun during the famine with the clearance of uneconomic smallholdings continued. Partible inheritance and subdivision of land amongst family members were phased out. Small farms did not disappear, though their numbers were reduced. Subsistence farming was still carried out in the west. In future, family holdings were to remain intact and be passed on through one heir, usually the eldest son. To facilitate this, emigration was imperative. Most families could only provide for the son who would inherit the farm. Usually only one daughter could hope for a dowry. Emigration was regarded almost as the duty of the siblings, since remittances from America would help to keep the family farm intact. There was not any real incentive to migrate within the country, to a town or city. Irish industry had collapsed in many towns and cities in the mid-nineteenth century, unable to face competition from cheaper imported goods from Britain and America. Urban workers, clerks, tradesmen, shop assistants and labourers joined the ranks of rural emigrants.

Single women, too, began emigrating in increasing numbers and after 1880 equalled or outstripped the number of emigrating men. This was another unique feature of Irish emigration. No other country in the world provided as many unaccompanied single female emigrants as did Ireland.

The desperate plight of those fleeing famine no longer characterised Irish emigration in subsequent years. But the pace of emigration kept up and emigration was still experienced as a kind of rupture: painful, frightening and involuntary. This comes through very clearly in contemporary accounts of emigration and in songs of emigration. A custom known as the "American wake" began around the middle of the nineteenth century. Neighbours and family would come to the house for a ritual of farewell that involved music, dancing, drinking and the singing of songs, which included songs of exile and emigration. "Wakes" often lasted all night and were witness to outpourings of grief and emotion. In *Twenty Years a Growing* Muiris Ó Súilleabháin gives an account of an American wake held for his sister Maura and another girl about to leave Great Blasket Island for Springfield, Massachusetts, in the 1920s. The passage money had been sent to Maura by her aunt in America. She went because: "Kate Peg is going and I have no need to stay here when all the girls are departing."[5] By this time many Blasket Islanders had already emigrated. Most of them had relatives in the States.

---

[5] Maurice O'Sullivan, *Twenty Years a Growing* (OUP, 1955), p. 216.

An article from the *Springfield Sunday Republican*, Massachusetts, 1952.
Great Blasket Island was fully evacuated in 1953.

Once the decision to go was made, homesickness and grief set in. Maura spent the days before she left crying and grieving for the life she would never see again. Of the wake Muiris reported:

> Young and old were gathered in the house, and though music and songs, dancing and mirth, were flying in the air, there was a mournful look on all within. No wonder, for they were all children of the one mother, the people of the Island, no more than twenty yards between any two houses, the boys and girls every moonlight night dancing on the sandhills or sitting together and listening to the sound of the waves from Shingle Strand; and when the moon would wane talking and conversing in the house of old Nell.[6]

This way of life was based on continuity and tradition and was communal rather than individualistic. In such a context emigration was a huge wrench; it was a kind of death and was mourned as such.

---

[6] *Ibid.*, p. 219.

The modern world had not much of a foothold in the life of the Blasket Islanders, but their culture was extraordinarily rich. Of the book *Twenty Years A Growing* (originally published in Irish as *Fiche Bliain ag Fás*) and the culture out of which it was written, the writer E.M. Forster had this to say:

> [It is] an account of Neolithic civilization from the inside. Synge and others have described it from the outside . . . but I know of no other instance where it has itself become vocal, and addressed modernity.[7]

While the Blasket community was unique in its state of uninterrupted civilisation, there were degrees to which this was true of all of rural Ireland in the nineteenth century. Modernisation was more advanced in some places where, as Irish historian Roy Foster said, "The values of the railway bookstall were replacing those of the street ballad." But the majority of those emigrating were leaving small farms and small communally organised societies where family, kin, and place were the focus of life. Frequently they did not even speak the language of "An t-Oileán Úr" – the "New Island", as America was called in Irish. They had no idea what to expect, having no experience of how modern society organised itself. Muiris Ó Súilleabháin had this vision of the New Island:

> It seemed to me that the New Island was before me with its fine streets and great high houses, some of them so tall that they scratched the sky; gold and silver out on the ditches and nothing to do but gather it. I see the boys and girls who were once my companions walking brightly and well contented.[8]

Songs of Exile and Emigration

There are many emigration songs warning of dangers and of intolerable homesickness. One is a song in Irish, "An t-Oileán Úr". In this account the singer has gone to America on the merest whim: "A thought came into my head, and I followed it with action, to slip away from my people and go over to America." He endures the hardships and terrors of the wilds until he meets some Irish people in a backwoods, telling us, interestingly, that he had to speak in English to them. Wonder of wonders, one of them is from his own home place. The joy of discovery, however, is quickly replaced by a longing to go home, even if it is to die: "I'd be lucky to be in Ireland even if stretched in a coffin, I'd find 'keeners' there to mourn me."[9]

Thousands of young Irish women and girls left for America. The Irish nationalist activist and writer Charles J. Kickham commemorated one such woman in the still-popular song "She lives beside the Anner". Again, no good comes of emigration. This "gentle Irish colleen" has to leave her (naturally) beautiful home place to support her family:

---

[7] *Ibid.*, Introduction.
[8] *Ibid.*, p. 236.
[9] Translation by Sean O Boyle, in *The Irish Song Tradition* (Ossian Publications, 1976), p. 79.

Sarah and Rita Keane of Caherlistrane, County Galway, recorded a song for *Bringing It All Back Home*, "A Stór Mo Chroí", which was often heard at American wakes at the turn of the century. The song is a love song for a child or perhaps a lover on the point of emigrating:

A stór mo chroí when you're far away,
from the home you will soon be leaving
tis many a time thro' the night and the day
that your heart it will soon be grieving.

There is an almost fatalistic acceptance that emigration is inevitable but heart-breaking. The loved one will be in the "stranger's land", as lonely and sad as the ones left at home. The vista is urban. There is mention of the "lights of their cities" and the "throng". Although there are "treasures golden", they will not satisfy and the emigrant will pine for the "long long ago".

Sarah and Rita sang this song in unison in the Sean Nós style, an unusual combination. Unaccompanied, melodic and spare, it avoids sentimentality, while painting a desolate picture of emigration. The air is traditional and predates the lyrics. A version of this song appears in a book published in 1915 entitled *Songs of the Gael*. Its editor, Father Padraig Breathnach, was so affected by the lyrics that he expressed the wish that "it will turn many an intending emigrant from his or her purpose of quitting their native land".

Another, earlier, song which attempts in a very forthright way to do this is "The Bonny Irish Maid", sung for *Bringing It All Back Home* by singers Fran McPhail, Phil Callery and Gerry Cullen. Solo singers in their own right, they sing in a choral style not traditional in Irish singing. They use this to great effect on their large repertoire of Irish traditional songs. The bonny Irish maid of the title attempts to turn her lover's intentions away from emigrating:

Oh many's the foolish youth she said
has gone to some foreign shore
leaving behind his own true love
perhaps to see no more.
It's in crossing of the Atlantic foam
Sometimes their graves are made
Oh stay at home love and do not roam
from your bonny Irish maid.

O brave, brave Irish girls!
We well may call you brave-
Sure the least of all your perils
Is the stormy ocean wave.
When you leave your quiet valleys,
And cross the Atlantic foam,
To hoard your hard won earnings
For the helpless ones at home.

This brave Irish girl reaches America but dies there, which causes the singer to reflect on "thy helpless fate, dear Ireland". In fact, most of these women and girls did not die tragic deaths but entered domestic service in the east-coast cities of America. They had many reasons to do so. Irish society after the famine provided women with three opportunities. Arranged marriage or entering a convent might have held out very limited measures of independence; spinsterhood, spent in domestic service or dependent on aging parents, offered none.

In America there was, at least, a measure of personal freedom, financial independence, and the possibility of personal choice in the matter of marriage partner. Not only was this not the case in Ireland, but the opportunities for marrying were very limited. The dowry system, the perpetuation of the family farm and mass emigration had meant that these opportunities did not exist.

By the 1880s eighty-one per cent of all Irish women immigrants in east-coast America were in domestic service. Most of them did marry there. A few returned home with their "dowries" earned, when it was remarked "they'd had enough of the washboard".

They all, men and women, sent millions of dollars home. This money helped to support the family, pay rent and ultimately bring brothers and sisters out. The fact that someone had relatives in America was in itself almost a reason for going.

"Ireland's helpless fate" was still uppermost in many emigrants' minds as the cause of emigration. Songs expressing nationalist sentiments were popular and these travelled to America with the emigrants. An incident recounted by John McClancy, who kept a diary of his voyage from Queenstown to New York, gives an impression of the feelings of the time. He left his home in County Clare in 1881 and boarded ship at Queenstown (now Cobh), County Cork. Queenstown was the most popular port of departure for emigrants in the south of Ireland. There was singing on deck at night amongst the sailors and the passengers, not all of whom were Irish:

One Irishman stood up and sang the shamrock so green and the decay of the rose the steward is an English man and when he heard English cut down he rushed and said he would not allow no more of this so the Irish persevered in singing until one Irish man for the good of the Irish to leave [sic] and sing in the bunk so each Irish man descended with black sticks cheering William O'Brien [a nationalist leader] and groaning Balfour [English

MP/Chief Secretary for Ireland] we were an over match for the English . . . so the brave man sang national songs until he made us sleep with them.[10]

There is no mention in John McClancy's diary of homesickness, but it is evident that the lullabies of the "brave Irish man" found a welcome response in the hearts of all those Irishmen on board. This identification with Ireland and with the "cause" of Ireland was kept alive on the New Island.

Kilkelly

Over one hundred and thirty years after his great grandfather left the small village of Kilkelly in County Mayo, Peter Jones found a bundle of letters sent to his great, great grandfather by his father in Ireland. The letters continued from 1860 until the old man's death in 1890. Though not exceptional in any way, they told of family news, births, deaths, sales of land, and bad harvests. They are reminders of the affection in which he was held, how he was missed and remembered by his family in Ireland. Over the course of time covered by the letters he married and had a family in America. One letter told him that his brother who emigrated to England had returned and was thinking of buying land. The final letter, written by another brother, informed him that his father, whom he had not seen for thirty years, had died; and in this way a letter breaks the last tangible link with home.

Peter Jones used his great, great grandfather's letters to write a song which he called "Kilkelly". The song was passed on to three Irish musicians living in the U.S.: Mick Moloney, Jimmy Keane and Robbie O'Connell are professional musicians who make their living playing music with a strong traditional base and who have made "Kilkelly" their own. It has become emblematic of the kind of immigrant culture they try to bring out in their music. As far as Moloney knows, it's the only song written "from the language of emigrant letters, not just in the Irish culture in America but, to the best of my knowledge, in any ethnic culture in this country".

The song has deeply affected all audiences. It touches in some fundamental way on the spirit of the emigrant experience. Whenever it is sung, listeners are moved to tears. Moloney describes "Kilkelly" as "the most eloquent and poignant tale of what it is like to be separated . . . the loneliness and the despair of it".

Throughout the nineteenth century and on into the twentieth century the haemorrhage continued. Between 1856 and 1921 over four million people emigrated, mainly to Britain. Most of these were young men and women, that section of the population with which every healthy country renews itself.

---

[10] Diary of John McClancy of Islandbawn, Miltown Malbay, County Clare (Nat. Lib. of Ireland MSS collection, MS 21666).

Their going reinforced the conservative social structure that developed after the famine and endured until the mid-1960s; the money they sent home helped sustain uneconomic farms and large families. The writer of the Kilkelly letters makes clear that if it wasn't for American money, they would not be able to keep going. Irish-Americans also helped perpetuate emigration not only by paying fares but by finding employment for relatives. Emigration is at the heart of the last two centuries of Irish history and its impact is only beginning to be understood. As historian Joe Lee wrote: "the imprint left by emigration will feature prominently as the archaeology of the modern Irish mind comes to be excavated."[11]

[11] Joe Lee, *Ireland 1912–1985* (CUP, 1989).

Four

The Wild Rovers

The immigrant group which contributed most to American folklore was the Irish.[1]

One way in which the movement of the Irish through America can be traced is through song. Many traditional songs, like "Rose Connolly", travelled with the immigrants. Around these immigrant experiences a new repertoire developed: railroad songs, lumberjack songs, work songs, songs of love and adventure, of exploitation, comic songs, nostalgic songs and songs of home. Many of these songs passed out of the preserve of the primary source ethnic group and entered the mainstream of American folk song. Just as the music of the Appalachian Scots-Irish was assimilated into the wider folk culture a century earlier, the music of mid-nineteenth-century Irish immigrants met and mingled with the music of other peoples. The two musical streams met on the railroads, in construction camps and farms, in travelling shows and in the music halls.

One of the most fruitful encounters in the history of modern folk song is that which occurred between the Irish and African-American music cultures.

The Working Life

The years immediately following the Great Famine were difficult for Irish emigrants to the east coast of America. They had endured famine at home, dangerous and pestilential sea voyages had killed thousands of them, and many were so broken in health and mind that they were unfit for work.

What work they could obtain was menial, hard and poorly paid. Immigrants worked in building construction, docking, machine shops, mines, and on canal and railroad construction. They lived in slum conditions in all the cities they settled in and their mortality from disease was high.

---

[1] A. Green Ed., *Railroad Songs and Ballads* (Library of Congress, Washington).

"Poor Paddy Works on the Railway"

In eighteen hundred and forty one
I put me cordroy britches on.
I put me cordroy britches on
To work upon the railway, the railway,
I'm weary of the railway,
Poor Paddy works on the railway.

This is one of the earliest recorded railroad songs and predates the famine exodus. It was already a popular song by the time the Union Pacific Railway Company laid the first westward track of the transcontinental railroad in 1863 from Omaha. At the same time the Central Pacific began moving eastward from Sacramento.

Thousands of Irish workers, many of them ex-soldiers who had fought in the American Civil War, worked on this epic construction. They travelled with the section gangs, living in work camps struck by the company along the route. Railroads and railroad construction spawned new song lore, stories and tunes which in time became a definitive part of American folk culture. From "The Wreck of the Old Ninety-Seven" to the "Chatanooga Choo Choo", the train is an evocative symbol of conquest and escape. In songs of the railroad Americans recognise themselves and their nation's history and folklore. There are work songs sung by the black section gangs to the rhythm of timber-felling, track-laying, hammering and spike-driving. There are songs of exploitation, of adventure and travelling, of outlaws and hobos. The image of the hobo riding the freight train is one which still appears in contemporary American popular song.

On the transcontinental line there were section gangs composed entirely of Irishmen. There were even section gangs which were made up of exclusively Irish-speaking Irishmen.

I landed in this country
a year and a month ago
To make my living at labouring work
to the railroad I did go.

The hero of this song, Mike Cahooley, is an exemplary railroad worker. He works so hard that he is made the boss of the section gang in a year:

I'm the walking boss of the whole railroad
for none I care a dang,
My name is Mike Cahooley
and I'm the boss of the section gang.

Mike Cahooley was typical of many of the Irish working on the transcontinental line. The work was hard; the pay was three dollars a day and the Irish were well regarded as workers. There were competitions between the eastward and westward workers to see who could lay the most track in a day and this speeded up construction. On average, three miles of track were laid a day and each line employed between eight and ten thousand workers. The Irish worked mainly on the Central Pacific; their work camps along the route grew into the towns and cities of the Midwest.

The two lines met at Promontory Utah on May 10, 1869, six years after work began. Within twenty years the last of the major railway construction would be finished and the frontier would no longer exist. Of this generation of Irish and Irish-Americans the great song collector Alan Lomax said:

> They brought little besides their strength, their wit, and their singing tradition with them, but without them America, and especially the railroads of America would never have been built . . . These lads were the principal singers in the lumber camps and on the canals. We know that they sang as they built the Erie, the Pennsylvania, and the Union Pacific.[2]

The Hills of Glenshee: Music of the Lumberjack

Pete Seeger is a singer usually associated with the five-string Appalachian banjo with which he accompanies himself, but there is a tune which he likes to play on the recorder called "The Hills of Glenshee". Seeger learned the air from an old lumberjack in the Catskill Mountains many years ago. It was, he says, originally a love song, but the words got lost along the way. The air had come to the lumberjack through his mother. Perhaps it originally had Irish words and so fell out of use with the adoption of English by Irish-speaking immigrants.

In the lumber camps, according to the collector Helene Stratman-Thomas, "the English speaking Irish seem to have been the principal bards". Certainly there are plenty of examples of songs of Irish derivation emanating from this source. An outlaw song, for example, "Brennan on the Moor", still well known in Ireland, has been collected in the lumber camps and in other parts of America. An American Library of Congress collection made in the lumber camp regions of Wisconsin includes a very interesting song with the title "I'll Sell my Hat, I'll Sell my Coat". In Ireland this song is known by its Irish language title "Siúil a Rún". It was recorded in the mid-1970s by the Donegal band Clannad, who have reworked many old traditional songs in an idiom incorporating folk, jazz and rock. The song dates from the seventeenth century and somehow endured in the living tradition in Ireland.

"Siúil a Rún" is one of a small number of traditional songs known as "macaronic". Macaronic songs include lines in both the Irish and English language, and date from a time and place

---

[2] John and Alan Lomax, *Best Loved American Folk Songs* (Grosset and Dunlop, 1947), Preface.

when the spoken language of the people was in transition from Irish to English. They derive in their construction from the compositions of mediaeval wandering bards who wrote vernacular and Latin macaronic songs; this, in turn, has been shown to have been an influence on Irish language folksong.

Sometimes in the Irish song the lines are alternately Irish and English, but in this case the chorus is in Irish and the verses in English. In the American version, the man promises to sell his hat and coat to "buy my wife a little flat boat". The Irish version has the girl promise to sell her spinning wheel to buy her love "a sword of steel".

To overcome the problem of the Irish-language chorus, the American version substitutes a nonsense-word rigmarole to approximate the sound of the Irish words. The first line of the chorus in Irish is "Siúil, siúil, siúil, a rún" ("Walk, walk, walk, my love"). In the American version this becomes "Shule, shule, shule – i rue", and continues in this vein, fitting nonsense words to the metre of the Irish chorus.

You're Welcome Here, Kind Stranger

In 1946 Helene Stratman-Thomas recorded Mrs Frances Perry of Black River Falls in Wisconsin singing "The Lakes of Ponchartrain". Stratman-Thomas noted that Mrs Perry learned the song from a family of settlers from Georgia. She also remarked that the song was to be found all over America "from Nova Scotia to Texas".

The hero of the song, a weary traveller in the southern states, falls in love with a beautiful Creole girl whom he meets on the lakes of Ponchartrain. She offers him the hospitality of her parents' house:

> *You're welcome here kind stranger*
> *our house is very plain*
> *But we never turn a stranger out*
> *On the Lakes of Ponchartrain.*

The song was recorded in Ireland nearly thirty years ago by Christy Moore, one of the country's most popular singers of ballads. He learned the song from the English traditional singer, Martin Carthy. In 1978 another Irishman then singing folk and traditional material, Paul Brady, recorded the song for his first solo album, which took its title "Welcome Here Kind Stranger" from a line in the song. It is supposed in Ireland that the young man is a soldier returning home from the American Civil War. Over two hundred thousand Irishmen did fight in the American Civil War, mostly on the Union side.

Whatever the young man's identity, the song's melancholy air has beguiled many Irish singers, including Liam Ó Maonlaí. Ó Maonlaí is a singer and musician whose involvement with The Hothouse Flowers band reflects eclectic musical influences running all the way from traditional Sean Nós singing in Irish (Ó Maonlaí is a fluent Irish speaker) to blues and rock. "I'm trained through Sean Nós," he reveals, "but that lends itself to an awful lot of modern rock, soul, blues singing . . . and lends itself to my own style of singing."

Something indefinable at the heart of "The Lakes of Ponchartrain" caught at Ó Maonlaí: "Paul Brady I heard singing that song . . . and I just fell in love with it . . . and we just had

to do it." He and the band recorded a fine version of the song for *Bringing It All Back Home*, Ó Maonlaí singing and accompanying himself at the piano with Leo Barnes providing a rich and evocative saxophone solo. Towards the end of the '90s he and Paul Brady worked on the song together and recorded a fine version of it for the Irish language music series "SULT", broadcast on the newly launched Irish language television channel TG4.

No Irish Need Apply

[The Irish] were the first major European unskilled ethnic group to come and settle in this land . . . a new land where they found that the old masters were still in the ascendancy. A lot of discrimination ensued and songs that mirror that abound . . . songs which show how the Irish were discriminated against and how negative stereotypes of the Irish abounded.

MICK MOLONEY

The arrival of large groups of unskilled, poor, famished and sometimes diseased Irish to the cities and towns of east-coast America horrified the Protestant establishment. This generation of Irish immigrants were to experience severe dislocation. The majority were from rural backgrounds unfamiliar with city life. They had no knowledge of the work practices and ethics of an industrialised society and a sizeable proportion had no English. Their world view is what is now described as pre-modern; their customs and social patterns were communalistic, non-literate and traditional.

The adjustment was painful and drawn out over generations. In the meantime they met with hostility, suspicion, bigotry and racism. Their arrival had coincided with the age of industrial expansion in America. They were the first emigrant group to provide the muscle and brawn that this demanded. Their first experience of work was of exploitation and discrimination.

In the coal mines they were paid low wages and were compulsorily bound to the company store and housing. Frequently they were hired for wages which were halved when too many turned up for the jobs. One Irish emigrant described the life of an Irish labourer in America as:

> despicable, humiliating and slavish . . . [There] was no love for him – no protection of life, [he] can be shot down, run through, kicked, cuffed, spat on – Irish b—— right, damn him.[3]

Everywhere the Irish settled, "No Irish Need Apply" notices followed. Researching in the American Library of Congress in the late forties, Pete Seeger came across two almost identical song texts on the subject of discrimination dating from this period in Irish-American history. He put them together and made a song he has been performing ever since: "No Irish Need Apply". The Irishman in the song is forced into the role assigned to him by caricaturists. Alternative role models have not yet emerged and he chooses to confront the oppressive employer who has posted a "No Irish Need Apply" notice.

> *Well I couldn't stand his nonsense*
> *So a hoult of him I took,*
> *And I gave him such a batin'*
> *As he'd get in Donnybrook*
> *And he hollered meela murder*
> *And to get away did try*
> *And he swore he'd never write again*
> *No Irish need apply.*

This outcome would seem to reflect wishful thinking rather than historical reality on the part of the songwriter. It is true, though, that violence was often the only weapon at the disposal of the oppressed worker during this period in labour history.

Labour unions were suppressed and many Irish workers got involved in secret societies. Many of them were familiar with this form of organisation in Ireland. One of the most famous secret organisations was set up in the anthracite fields of Pennsylvania in the 1860s. The anthracite miners were forced to work under abominable conditions and were prevented from striking or negotiating with their bosses. They retaliated by forming the Molly Maguires. This organisation was responsible for the murders of mine managers and informers. They were eventually caught and nineteen of them hanged.

---

[3] Kerby Miller, *Emigrants and Exiles – Ireland and the Irish Exodus to North America* (OUP, 1985), p. 323.

By the 1880s labour organisations were in a strong enough position to establish the American Federation of Labour. By the turn of the century the AFL represented seventy-five per cent of all organised labour in the U.S. The Irish predominated in the early labour unions. Irish women were notably active. The famous "Mother Jones", who organised for the miners' union, was Mary Harris of County Cork. Lenora O'Reilly organised the garment workers of New York, and Elizabeth Gurley Flynn became one of the most radical and able labour organisers of the twentieth century.

Cartoon Paddy

[The Irish] were the first group, except native Americans and blacks, about whom there grew unflattering, mordant, and hostile stereotypes.[4]

The social lives of the Irish repelled the city elders; their tendency to congregate in ghettos gave them the name "Shanty Irish". Their drinking, riotous wakes, dances and quarrelling brought down the wrath of policemen and magistrates. Out of their lives and occupations came the "Paddy" and "Biddy" stereotypes which dogged Irish Americans for generations.

The ape-like Irishman with his clay pipe was a standard depiction. Portrayed in a variety of guises designed to demonstrate his stupidity, barbarity, drunkenness, shiftlessness and lawlessness, "Pat" was a stock cartoon character.

A cartoon entitled "Uncle Sam's Lodging House" shows amongst all the other well-behaved representatives of America's immigrant nations one brawling Irish ape-man in his bunk. He is nursing a bottle of whiskey and "giving the finger" to his host, Uncle Sam. This cartoon appeared in *Puck*, a popular weekly magazine, in June 1892. Underneath, the editorial read:

The raw Irishman in America is a nuisance, his son a curse. They never assimilate; the second generation shows an intensification of all the bad qualities of the first . . . they are a burden and a misery to this country.

---

[4] John and Selma Appel, *Pat-Riots to Patriots, American Irish in Caricature and Comic Art* (Michigan State University Museum, 1990).

This attitude prevailed until the turn of the century. By then the stereotype had evolved into a variety of types: Paddy the feckless, charming amusing fellow, Paddy the rogue and Paddy the joker. Those Irish who had by now managed to climb a rung or two up the social ladder were characterised as "lace curtain Irish" and their petit-bourgeois pretensions were ridiculed. From the 1850s onwards weekly magazines like *Puck* and the new newspaper comic strips developed their stock of Irish stereotypes. The bestial denizen of earlier caricatures became the cop, the hod-carrier, the washer-woman, the colleen, the saloon-keeper, the ward politician and the Irish drunk. Of these only the Irish drunk and the Irish cop persist to this day.

Shamrocks, Shillelaghs and Shenanigans

Irish Americans, particularly the second generation Irish, participated eagerly in the new American mass culture. It was a Casey after all who was at bat, a Sullivan and a Corbett in the ring, and Harrigans, Harts, Rooneys and Cohans romping on vaudeville stages.[5]

The variety stage, vaudeville, burlesque and slapstick were the popular entertainments of immigrants in nineteenth-century American cities. From the 1850s in every city, music halls offered several different shows. Music hall belonged to immigrants. On the music-hall stage they heard their own accents, saw their own world, their own hopes and dreams of America.

Audiences were characterised by their lack of restraint and their involvement with the show. They sang along, they ate, laughed and roared at the performers whom they knew by name. Stock Irish characters took to the music hall stage early on. They were never objects of racist ridicule. In a way, the music hall and vaudeville show gave back to immigrants what the crude caricatures of comic strips and cartoons took away. Stage Irishmen like "Throw him down Mc Closkey" and "Mc Ginty" landed in all sorts of scrapes but came through, often at the expense of the uppity Yankee.

Edward Harrigan was an acclaimed writer for the variety stage. With songwriter Dave Braham and actor Tony Hart he enjoyed decades of uninterrupted popularity. Harrigan was the grandson of Irish immigrants and had grown up in an Irish slum in Manhattan. At this time in the 1860s there was more Irish spoken there than English. When he was a boy, twenty-six per cent of the population of New York, about 133,000 people, were Irish born. About one third of them were Irish speakers.

From the 1870s to the end of the century Harrigan produced plays for the variety stage. They featured the beggars, maids, street-sellers, landlords, hod-carriers, Germans, Jews and Irish of the city of immigrants. "I have sought above all," he said, "to make all my plays like pages from actual life."

There was a strong Irish element to the songs in Harrigan shows. A song from the Harrigan and Hart show *The Merry Malones*, called "Danny by my Side", was a favourite of the Irish-

---

[5] Timothy J. Meagher, "From Paddy to Studs" in *Irish American Communities 1880–1920* (Greenwood Press, 1986).

American Governor of New York, Alfred E. Smith. He sang at a ceremony to celebrate the fiftieth anniversary of the completion of the Brooklyn Bridge. The bridge owed more than a little to the labour of Irish workers, many of whom died during its construction.

Irish music was also assimilated into variety. An early encounter was with the music of black America. This creative fusion produced the first dance routines of the early variety show entertainers. Thomas Dartmouth "Daddy" Rice is credited with marrying an Irish fiddle tune to an African-American shuffle dance, thereby "inventing" the "soft-shoe shuffle" routine which became the popular minstrel dance "Jump Jim Crow". An Irishman by the name of Dan Emmet was one of the first blackface minstrels and wrote "Dixie" and the "Blue Tail Fly". This was a staple minstrel routine, and was a typical African-American and Irish mixture of Irish hornpipe and the black tune "Jim Crack Corn". Out of this interaction evolved the "buck and wing" and "soft-shoe shuffle" steps which became the basic figures in all dance routines in music hall variety shows.

These pioneers of variety would have agreed with Edward Harrigan when he said that he returned to the themes of runaway slaves and Irish immigrants because the Irish and the African-Americans were the two races who cared most about song and dance.

As a young man, the first generation Irish American Jerry Cohan made several appearances in Harrigan and Hart shows. He was the son of Irish famine immigrants and was an acclaimed traditional dancer. The dance act he developed was based on the jigs and reel figures of Irish traditional dance. His travelling show, called the *Hibernicon*, was a rag-bag of sketches, comic acts, and song and dance routines and was immensely popular with immigrant audiences everywhere. He also toured with his wife and two children as "The Four Cohans". His son, George M. Cohan, was to become an American archetype – the "Song and Dance Man". In Cohan's hands, music hall severed its links with immigrant culture and became American.

Yankee Doodle Dandy

"Yankee Doodle Dandy" appeared in the 1904 show *Little Johnny Jones*. This song and "Give my Regards to Broadway" were two smash hits of the year. The show was written, directed and produced by George M. Cohan, who also played the lead.

He claimed to have been born on July 4, although his birth certificate said July 3. He was in all other respects a Yankee Doodle Boy, the grandson of Irish immigrants who had fled the famine. In two generations he came to embody an essentially American spirit: plucky, enterprising and patriotic.

Cohan, in his show *George Washington Junior*, produced another hit on this very theme, "You're a Grand Old Flag". His shows sold out and succeeded in spite of the attacks of critics in the quality papers. He was criticised for being "vulgar, cheap and blatant", but Bob Callahan described him as "nothing more or less than the very spirit of turn-of-the-century America itself, with the throttle pushed all the way to the floor . . . ".[6]

George M. Cohan's contribution was significant in purely musical terms. His dance routines, songs and even his posture on stage were all imitated. His "Give My Regards to Broadway" and "Yankee Doodle Dandy" became American anthems.

In "Thousands are Sailing" Philip Chevron celebrated Cohan's contribution to American popular culture both as a songwriter and as an "Irish bard", Times Square's very own Irishman.

> *And we said goodnight to Broadway*
> *giving it our best regards*
> *tipped our hats to Mr Cohan*
> *dear old Time Square's favourite bard.*

When Irish Eyes are Smiling

The musicians and music performed on the music-hall stage in the nineteenth century entertained an immigrant audience with the stuff of their own lives. Irish material was worked into the plots, songs and dialogue in a way that reflected the new reality of immigrant life. By the end of the century some of these stage Irishisms were already a throwback to an earlier immigrant reality. They embarrassed the upwardly mobile Irish on their way out to the suburbs where ethnic identities were not so pronounced.

Audiences were no longer eating and drinking in the stalls and roaring at the players on the stage. Few Irish-Americans needed to be reminded of the reality of tenement life as they were about to take their first step out of it. Like James Tyrone in Eugene O'Neill's play *Long Day's Journey into Night*, they had long memories. They knew "the value of a dollar and the fear of the poorhouse".

They wanted to forget the bad times and remember what good times there were. Good times could also be manufactured. Tin Pan Alley (the collective name for the music publishing business based around New York's 28th Street) was happy to oblige. Its songsmiths churned out thousands of "Oirish" numbers from the quaint to the downright sentimental. From this source came a song which entered the repertoire of every Irish tenor, "Mother Machree", written by one of Tin Pan Alley's principal balladeers, Chauncey Olcott. He also wrote what Mick Moloney describes as "the anthem of mainstream Irish America" – "When Irish Eyes are Smiling".

> *When Irish hearts are happy*
> *All the world seems bright and gay,*
> *And when Irish eyes are smiling*
> *Sure they steal your heart away.*

---

[6] Bob Callahan, *The Big Book of American-Irish Culture* (Viking, 1987), p. 14.

"Mother Machree" was the stage favourite of the internationally acclaimed Irish tenor John McCormack, who toured America in the first two decades of the twentieth century. McCormack himself was at the centre of an incident which revealed the ambivalence at the core of Irish-American self-perception. The renowned Irish piper Patsy Touhey travelled the U.S. on the variety circuit in stage shows like the Cohans' *Hibernicon*. In addition to playing the uilleann pipes, he performed a comic Mick-and-Pat routine of the stage-Irish sort. He and McCormack were on the same bill at the New Orleans Fair in 1911. McCormack was so incensed by Touhey's display of paddywhackery that he made it a condition of his contract that Touhey's act be taken out of the set.

Irish emigrants to America in the late nineteenth and early twentieth centuries were better equipped to cope with the life that lay ahead of them. They were better educated than the Famine Irish who came before them. They joined an established Irish-American network of relations and neighbours. Using these connections enabled them to find jobs and accommodation. They were predisposed to assimilate. The Catholic Church in America had long put in place a programme of full American integration realised through a highly organised parish system which promulgated, amongst other things, the virtues of patriotic allegiance to America.

There were other emigrants who travelled to America with no English and from backgrounds thousands of cultural years away from American life. Some of this generation never assimilated. There were always those who never wavered in their allegiance to Ireland and all that entailed culturally and politically. Nationalism of every hue, from radical revolutionary to constitutionalist, found a home in Irish America and still does. Of this the Irish historian Roy Foster says that Ireland "claimed a fiercely and unrealistically obsessive identification from its emigrants". It must be said that this "obsessive identification" ensured that a musical tradition long in the doldrums in Ireland would stay alive in America and endure to go back home.

Eventually the Pat and Mick stereotypes vanished from the scene. Central Casting replaced them with new characters. The Irish cop is one "stock character". which has persisted right into the twenty-first century, in fiction at least. Gene Kelly in *Going My Way* is the epitome of the celluloid Irish priest; Jimmy Cagney, his dark alter ego the Irish gangster, who dies screaming for his mother. These fictive Irish then influenced the way in which Ireland and things Irish came to be imagined by very many Irish Americans generations away from the source culture. In this process a song like "I'll Take You Home Again Kathleen" or "Irish Eyes", written in America by songwriters with no access to or knowledge of Irish music, came to represent not only Irish music but also "Irishness".

Five

The Jig of Life

We sit up there on the stage and play concerts . . . but people will invariably say
at the end of the night: "God, we were dying to get up and dance."

FRANKIE GAVIN OF DE DANNAN

The instrumental tradition of music of Ireland is mainly comprised of dance music and largely dates from the eighteenth century.

At the outset it was part of a rich and active tradition of dancing which reached its peak of popularity towards the end of the eighteenth century and maintained it for nearly a century, despite

Dancing the Irish jig: an illustration by Forester in *L'Illustration*, 1894.

the devastation of the Great Famine and the disapproval of the Catholic Church. The primary function of a musician in this milieu was to provide music for dancing, although exemplary musicians were also valued for their playing alone.

In the nineteenth century Irish traditional music first began to separate from the dance. This important development shaped the future of traditional music in America and in Ireland.

The Irish Tradition of Dance

Damhsa and *rince*, used interchangeably to mean dance in Irish, are both borrowings from English. Jigs and reels, the two main dances, derive from Italian and Anglo-Saxon traditions respectively. Accounts of life in seventeenth and early eighteenth century Ireland report dancing as a popular activity. Round, or group, dances – where the dancers formed a long line or a circle – seem to have been in vogue, but we have very little idea of what these dances looked like or how the music sounded.

As Mícheál Ó Súilleabháin has pointed out, the occupation of the mainly peasant population was subsistence farming, with its concomitant enforced leisure time in the quiet season. This time was partly filled with music and dancing. Central to this eighteenth and nineteenth century dance culture was the travelling dancing master. The arrival of the itinerant dancing master was eagerly awaited in these communities.

The dancing master worked a regular route around townlands and parishes, stopping at one for a few weeks before moving on to the next. Dancing masters respected each other's territories, although there was a competitive aspect to the securing of a particular parish. The dancing master would put up in the house of a local farmer or spend a night in turn with each of his pupils, who were the usual mixed bag of the naturally gifted, the competent and the clumsy. His arrival meant days of more or less continuous dancing and one or two "big nights" or gala affairs of entertainment and drinking. The eighteenth century traveller in Ireland, Arthur Young, noted:

> Dancing . . . is almost universal in every cabbin. Dancing masters . . . travel the country from cabbin to cabbin with a piper or blind fiddler: and the pay is sixpence a quarter. It is an absolute system of education.[1]

A feature of Irish dancing which has remained the same to this day is the particular stance of the dancer. There is no movement of the body above the hips. Relatively little floor space is covered by the dancer or dancers. The solo dancer often danced on a single plank of wood or a door taken off its hinges for the purpose, creating an effect described by Breandán Breathnach:

> The good dancer danced, as it were, underneath himself, trapping each note of the music on the floor.[2]

---

[1] Breandán Breathnach, *Folk Music and Dances of Ireland*, p. 49.
[2] *Ibid.*, p. 53.

The basic dances taught were the jig and reel, which incorporated stamping, shuffling, grinding, skipping and hopping steps. A good dancer would be taught pieces for solo performance incorporating these steps, and also special exhibition dances known as set dances. Talented pupils often went on to become dancing masters themselves. The other pupils were taught round or group dances, because dancing had a social function and was a popular pastime at weddings, festivals, and other occasions. Dancing was completely interwoven into the fabric of community life. It came as naturally as talking, story-telling, or singing, and remained a feature of rural life for over three hundred years.

In his diary of his voyage on an emigrant ship from Queenstown, County Cork, to New York in 1881, John J. McClancy mentions the preferred ways of passing time on board.

"The Ould Irish Jig" – from a 1906 postcard.

About eve . . . we had music and dance of all kinds we had great fun in the Germans the way they dance is wheeling around always like we would dance a polka . . . When we come up in the morning we dont go down until night the boys and girls are to and fro over the deck we have great games dancing and singing . . . Wednesday morning there was heavy rain and fog thunder and lightening we remained down dancing for most part of the day.[3]

The Music of the Dance

Irish music is not merely not European, it is quite remote from it. It is, indeed, closer to some forms of oriental music. The first thing we must do, if we are to understand it, is to forget about European music. Its standards are not Irish standards; its style is not Irish style; its forms are not Irish forms.[4]

The first thing that must be said about Irish traditional music is that it does not use the same scales as European or Western music of the last two centuries. These are the major and minor scales on which

[3] Diary of John McClancy, Islandbawn Miltown Malbay, County Clare (National Library of Ireland MSS collection, MS 21666).
[4] Seán Ó Riada, *Our Musical Heritage*, p. 20.

all Western music is based. A scale is a collection of notes with set intervals of tones or half-tones between them. In Western music the scale used is a seven-gapped scale of eight notes called an octave. In tonic sol-fa, a system of naming the notes of the scale used to teach singing, they are known as doh, ray, mi, fah, soh, lah, te, and doh. The tonic, or bottom, note normally gives the scale its key, but the notes of the scale will have the same relationship to each other regardless of key. The minor scale differs from the major in one respect: the interval between the second and third note is a half-tone, rather than a full-tone, interval.

Irish music, on the other hand, is modal. In the modal system it is possible to have seven scales: Irish music uses four of these. All this means is that there is a different, more interesting tonal character to traditional music thanks to possibilities which do not apply in Western music. The traditional music of England and America is also modal.

Western ears are more attuned to harmonic music where notes are sounded together as in chords or harmony singing. Irish music is essentially monophonic (single sound) and depends on a single decorated melody line.

In Western art-music there is theme, variation, and resolution. In traditional music, particularly dance music, the tune can be repeated as often as desired and the last phrase of one tune leads naturally to the beginning of another (as demonstrated in Chapter 1 by whistle player Mary Bergin using the final note of the first reel as a bridge to a second).

What tune goes with what is left to the discretion of the players in session. Equally, when and where the music stops is for the players to decide, though always within the structural constraints of the tune. The music is not developed, resolved and brought to a conclusion in the classical sense. The Irish composer Seán Ó Riada described this as the circular nature of Irish music:

> the graph of real life. Every day the sun rises, every day it sets. Every day possesses the same basic characteristics, follows the same fundamental pattern, while at the same time each day differs from the last in its ornamentation of events.[5]

So with circularity goes ornamentation. Without it the music would be predictable and monotonous, the same each time it is played. Ornamentation makes it possible for a tune to be fresh. It is still the same tune, as a day is still a day, but is different in the way that one day is from another.

Ornamentation offers three possibilities. One is to decorate the tune by adding trills, triplets, or grace notes. The second is to change the order of the melody, but not so much that the tune is bent out of shape. The third is to make slight variations in the rhythm or metre of the piece. There is a vocabulary which musicians use to describe these effects: cranning, rolling, and double-stopping are some of the terms. Mastering the melody line is only the beginning of learning how to play traditional music.

---

5   *Ibid.*, p. 21.

Some musicians like to use other musicians' "settings" of tunes rather than attempt to arrange these themselves. This also demands a lot of the player, bearing in mind that any one player may have over two hundred tunes in his or her repertoire. It is also easy to see how what in Western music would be a very short melody is laden with infinite possibilities.

Fiddler Paddy Glackin described a reel, "The Glen Road to Carrick", which he recorded with his brothers Seamus and Kevin for *Bringing It All Back Home*, as:

> a timeless tune; that's a tune one would never get fed up of for the simple reason it's such an interesting tune; there are five parts in it and there are so many possibilities within that that makes it so interesting.

A musician's ability to ornament a tune is very highly regarded and, as Seán Ó Riada said, this kind of musician is "a creative contributor to the tradition. He makes it grow and develop".[6] Irish music, then, is circular, melodic and ornamented. It makes little use of dynamics – there is no loud and soft, little vibrato. The musical quality arises from the melody, the ornamentation of the melody and the instrument used.

Frankie Gavin and Yehudi Menuhin recording an Irish hornpipe in New York for *Bringing It All Back Home*.

---

[6] Sean Ó Riada, "Our Musical Heritage".

In the days before recorded music, motor cars and mass communications, a traditional musician learned tunes locally. Each region had its own style of playing its own particular tunes. Sometimes a preference for a certain instrument developed, such as the leaning toward fiddles or flutes in Sligo, or concertinas in Clare. There are very few players left in Ireland who are exclusively regional in their playing, like the brothers John and Paddy Killourhy.

They learned their music from neighbours in their native west Clare, a county famous for traditional music and players and for a strongly marked regional music tradition. The Killourhy repertoire and style was not influenced by players from other parts of Ireland, nor by radio or records, mainly because the Killourhys never moved outside their own locality: "We've played for country dances all our lives," says John Killourhy. Playing and dancing were inseparable for them.

The Dances

The most popular dances are jigs and reels and these constitute the majority of tunes. Jigs, according to Breandán Breathnach, are the oldest dance tunes in Ireland. Jigs come in three forms: single jigs, double jigs, and slip jigs, depending on the arrangement of notes within the bar. The reel is by far the most popular playing tune because of its fast, fluid rhythm. It's also common to the whole country. Reels are

Brothers Paddy and John Killourhy in their County Clare home. They
have been players of traditional music for house dances all their lives.

played in 4/4 time with two groups of four quavers to the bar. Many reel tunes are Scottish in origin. The popular reel "Miss Mc Leods", for example, is common to the Scots, Irish and American traditions.

The hornpipe dance is of English origin. Like the reels, hornpipes are in 4/4 time, played slower, and more heavily accented. Hornpipes are not so plentiful as jigs and reels but they are in every player's repertoire.

Until recently slides and polkas were mainly heard in the south and west of the country in Clare, Cork, Limerick and Kerry, and were especially associated with one particular area of the country, Sliabh Luachra, on the Cork-Kerry border. Excepting musicians from this area, slides and polkas are not as frequently played as reels and jigs. The polka is in 2/4 time and the slide in 6/8.

Highlands are associated with the regional playing of Donegal in the far north-west of the country. This county had a lot of contact, through seasonal migration, with neighbouring Scotland, and music came back along this route. The highland is known in Scotland as the highland fling and is a national dance. In Donegal the tunes were adapted and enjoyed great popularity with fiddle players. Altan's Mairéad Ní Mhaonaigh is a Donegal fiddle player, and describes highlands as "slower reels; they're still in 4/4 time like a reel would be but . . . slower . . . the rhythm is more measured".

It is taken for granted in traditional music today that dance music is instrumental music. Alongside the performance of dance music as a purely instrumental form is a relatively new dance culture which enjoyed a major revival in the last decades of the twentieth century. This culture embraces all forms of traditional dance, from the competitive solo and group types to Sean Nós, or old style, solo or exhibition dancing to "set" dancing. Set dances are essentially group dances based on quadrilles where two sets of two couples dance facing each other.

Set dancing was in decline when the organisers of the Willie Clancy Summer School (one of the best known and most frequented traditional music summer schools in Ireland) began set dancing workshops in the seventies. These quickly established themselves as one of the most popular events in the summer school programme. From such beginnings grew a national and, indeed, international network of classes, events and competitions. Dancing masters once more travelled the country teaching the sets in school halls, pubs and other venues. Old set dances not seen in decades were revived by a new generation of dancers. Where the dancing had not entirely died out, it received a shot in the arm from the upsurge of interest in the old "sets". Aspiring dancers began to arrive in areas like Sliabh Luachra and the Dingle penninsula, anxious to acquire the figures of the set from local dancers.

Musicians had to respond and in time bands and individual players emerged to deal with the demand for players to accompany the dancers. For some musicians, like Seamus Begley, little had changed except that now there were more dancers around. In his native Gaeltacht community of Corca Dhuibhne in west Kerry it was expected that the local musician would play for dancers. He teamed up with guitarist Steve Cooney to form what would become one of the best-known partnerships in traditional music in the eighties and nineties. Paradoxically, out of this involvement with dance music and dancers Begley and Cooney became popular concert performers and their recording *Meitheal* a classic album of the nineties. Cooney's rhythmic and syncopated guitar style, which developed out of the dance music of

Seamus Begley

Stephen Cooney

west Kerry, has been a major influence on contemporary accompaniment in Irish traditional music, particularly amongst younger players. The popularity of set dancing has levelled off since its peak in the early nineties but still maintains a strong presence in mainstream traditional music culture.

The Church and Dancing

Dancing is . . . a thing which leads . . . to bad thoughts and evil actions . . . it is dancing that excites the desires of the body . . . In the dance are seen frenzy and woe, and with dancing thousands go to the black hell.

DONAL O'COLMAIN, Parish Priest, 1670[7]

For nearly three hundred years the Catholic Church in Ireland inveighed against their parishioners' main recreational pastime – dancing. From the seventeenth century onwards, the Catholic clergy in many parts of the country actively waged campaigns against dancing. Often the supreme authority in local communities, they had the power to invoke the ultimate anathema of excommunication. Their opposition was stated to be on moral grounds. Dancing was said to be sinful because it led to promiscuity and drunkenness.

"Pattern" or "Patron" days, in particular, came in for strong clerical censure. These were originally the feast days of a local saint or patron and were held at a "holy" place, such as a well associated with the saint. After a certain amount of praying and penance, the assembly got down to

---

[7] Brian O Cuiv (Ed.), *Parliament na Mban* (Dublin, 1952), trans. by Breandán Breathnach.

celebrating the day with music, dancing and drinking. According to Sir Henry Piers, who observed a Pattern day in 1682, "the day is spent as if they celebrated the Bacchanalia, rather than the memory of a pious saint".[8] Sir Henry found the dancing "lewd and obscene". One hundred years later, another traveller in Ireland, John Carr, found the Sunday practice of dancing entirely charming: "A spirit of gaiety shines upon every hour, the bagpipe is heard, and every foot is in motion."[9] The bishop of Cashel and Emly in 1796 threatened that if any behaviour other than strict religious devotions was observed on the Patron day in his diocese, the feast day would be suppressed. Those who had transgressed by singing, dancing, or merrymaking would be excommunicated.

There is little evidence to connect dancing with debauchery, although Pattern days did frequently get out of hand. Breandán Breathnach pointed out that most of the dancing was solo dancing and, when there were group dances, the boys and girls did not hold one another.[10] Captain Francis O'Neill, the great collector of Irish music in America, remained bitter to the end of his days about the way the clergy had "capriciously and arbitrarily" suppressed the music in his home place near Bantry in west Cork. He considered their opposition "senseless hostility" since all dances were held in public, often in the open air, and always "among friends and neighbours".

Whatever the reasons, clerical opposition and interference continued right up to the middle of last century. Stories about priests breaking up house parties, barn dances, open-air dancing, beating up musicians and breaking instruments abound. In Captain O'Neill's parish of Caherea in west Cork, the local piper, who was blind and made his living from piping, was forced into the poorhouse in Bantry after the parish priest banned crossroads and house dances. This took place around 1860 and may have been one of the reasons that young Francis O'Neill, a brilliant musician, took off for America four years later at the age of sixteen. There was no more music at home.

A typical example of clerical interference is related in this account of an incident which took place in the west of Ireland in 1919. A piper called Ruane visited a place called Teach a Gheata (Gate House) every Sunday. In the words of a local man, Tomas Laighleis:

> No old person, man or woman who had a hop in them failed to come. There was no fighting or trouble, no man was seen drunk there, no girl ever lost her reputation there . . . The parish priest with one terrible sermon from the altar stopped them.
>
> Ruane was told what had happened and what the priest had said. He burst out crying, turned on his heel and went home. Ruane never came another Sunday there or any other piper ever again . . .

---

[8] Breandán Breathnach, "The Church and Dancing in Ireland" (*Dal gCais*, 1982).
[9] *Ibid.*
[10] *Ibid.*

Crossroads dances were a feature of social life in rural Ireland well into the twentieth century.
This photograph was taken in Glendalough, County Wicklow.

The priests were not always successful in their endeavours. Great care was taken not to let clergy know when a dance was happening, and look-outs would be posted on the road to warn the assembly to break up. The clergy made up for being kept in the dark by preaching fiery sermons. John Killourhy recalled from his own youth:

> Well the old priests were a fright to God, I might as well tell you the truth. They were desperate.
> They were giving desperate sermons . . . they were telling the people they were damned – they'll
> go down to Hell. The divil will drag them away without telling them they were damned.

Sometimes dance music was able to avoid or resist interdict and of course not all priests were so violently set against dancing. Indeed, many priests shared a common cultural background with their parishioners and were even musicians themselves, and so were inclined to turn a blind eye.

The house dances, patterns, and crossroads dances were the means by which the dance-music tradition was kept alive. Having survived the famine and clerical anathema, the death blow was nonetheless dealt to the tradition by a lethal combination of both Church and State.

In the twenties another dance craze hit Ireland. This enthusiasm was for "modern" dances like waltzes, foxtrots, and so on. The dances were held in commercial dance halls beyond the reach of clergy and moral watchdogs of any kind. The popularity of this kind of dancing incensed not only the clergy but other elements in society who saw in these "foreign" dances a threat to the moral wellbeing of the entire youth of the country. By the 1930s both Church and government were denouncing dancing from pulpit, press, school and political platforms. The Public Dance Halls Act of 1935 required all public dance halls to be licensed and to operate under prescribed conditions. The priests used the Act as a way of finishing off the house dances, with the aid of the police.

In the thirties house dances would often be held in conjunction with raffles or card-game tournaments. This was the time of the so-called Economic War in Ireland. Exports of farm produce to Britain were suspended and Irish farmers, especially small farmers, were badly hit. The house dances or "soirées", as they were known, were ways of raising money for people in the community who were in financial trouble. Suggestions that the proceeds were going to fund illegal organisations like the Irish Republican Army and the priests' contentions that they were occasions of sin led to their closure. The legal pretext was that house dances constituted an infringement of the Public Dance Halls Act.

Purely private house dances with no raffle or tournament aspect were also harried out of existence. Junior Crehan, a fiddle player from County Clare where house dances were very popular, remembers:

> The clergy started to build the parochial halls to which all were expected to go and the Government collected 25 per cent of the ticket tax. In these halls modern dance bands played a different type of dancing – Foxtrot, One Step, and Shimmy Shake . . . the dance halls were not natural places of enjoyment; they were not places for traditional music, story-telling and dancing; they were unsuitable for passing on traditional arts. The Dance Halls Act had closed our schools of tradition and left us a poorer people.[11]

The priests' work was undoubtedly helped along by the emigration which resumed after the First World War and continued unabated until the sixties. In addition, radio broadcasting had started and the gramophone had arrived. The house dances would have been affected by these developments in any event.

The Céilí Band

Irish dance music did not disappear. It couldn't beat the dance halls, so it joined them. The céilí band was born out of a compromise between modernity and tradition. The Irish word "céilí" refers to the custom of neighbours gathering together in one or another's house for conversation and company, story-telling and maybe (but not necessarily) dancing and music. The word can be used in English as an adjective, as in the expression "céilí band", or as a noun to describe an organised dance. The first céilí dances were organised by nationalistically minded emigrants in London at the beginning of the twentieth century.

---

[11] "Junior Crehan Remembers" (*Dal gCais*, 1977).

The idea for the céilí was borrowed from Scottish revivalist groups which organised dances featuring settings of Scottish dances. The dancing at these events owed more to Scotland than to Ireland, resembling the group dances of that country and not the set and solo dances of the country-house gatherings.

Irish cultural activities were very popular with the Irish in Britain around this time and there was also a lot of travelling between the two countries. In post-Independence Ireland, there was now a State-sanctioned revival in Irish music and culture generally. The prototype for what became the céilí band emerged amongst Irish emigrant groups in Britain and America and was then adopted in the home country. The classic line-up of a céilí band was fiddle, flute, accordion, piano and drums. The music, to adapt itself to the dance hall, had to become louder and have a heavier and more rhythmic backing. Many of the musicians were solo traditional players in their own right and competed as solo players at the Fleadheanna (traditional music competitions) which began in the fifties.

The céilí bands endured for forty years; although there are still céilí bands performing in Ireland today, their heyday is past. The céilí dances, group dances like "The Walls of Limerick" and "The Siege of Ennis" where the dancers faced each other in long lines, and the eight and sixteen-hand reels were replaced by the "sets". The sets are dances performed by four couples who dance face to face, or facing out and holding hands. These correspond to the sets of the country-house dances and do not require a band.

Many purists decried the céilí bands as a sell-out. Many of the céilí were run by stridently nationalist and (ironically) Catholic groups. In many cases their objectives were not so much to provide music and entertainment as to preserve Irish youth from foreign, "immoral" influences. As the sixties and seventies approached, many young people were repelled or bored by céilí dancing. Seán Ó Riada, whose work as a composer and innovator in the field of traditional music is described in detail in Chapter 7, thought the céilí band an abomination.

> The most important principles of traditional music – the whole idea of variation, the whole idea of the personal utterance – are abandoned. Instead everyone takes hold of a tune and belts away at it with as much relation to music as the buzzing of a bluebottle in an upturned jam jar.[12]

Seán Ó Riada delivered himself of this opinion on a radio programme entitled "Our Musical Heritage" in 1962. He had his own ideas about group-playing of Irish music, which he had already begun to put into practice. What he was doing would profoundly change the face of Irish traditional music.

In their defence, Barry Taylor wrote of céilí bands:

> [Ó Riada] had failed to understand the fundamental role of the music, and, therefore, of its practitioners. Any questions of "personal utterance" and "variation" are entirely secondary to the musicians' main role: that is to provide a solid rhythmic base for the dancers.[13]

---

12 Seán Ó Riada, *Our Musical Heritage*, p. 74.
13 Barry Taylor, "Irish Ceílídh Bands: A Break with Tradition?" (*Dal gCais*, 1984).

As one traditional player remarked, "you didn't play to be listened to, you played to be danced to . . . There was no such thing as a player coming into a house and expecting people to sit down, listening to him."

Dancing Music/Listening Music

It is true that the céilí bands kept dance music alive for dancers, brought it to a wider audience than otherwise would have been possible, and gave a platform and a training to young players. Until the twentieth century the dance music of Ireland was played for community dancing, at house parties, patterns, weddings, wakes, and so on. The one exception to this rule was when a player of renowned virtuosity played. He or, more rarely, she was listened to. These players became, in Ciarán MacMathúna's words, "musicians in their own right", no longer defined by the dance. They were exceptional, though, and it was demanded of the rest that they perform for the dance.

> God be good to Seamus Ennis, but if you danced when Seamus Ennis was playing you were soon told to stop, particularly by Seamus; this was music for listening even though it was dance music.[14]

In the 1920s a development took place which changed the relationship between musicians and dancers forever. It happened in America and it had a profound effect on the future course of Irish traditional music both in Ireland and America. It was the invention of the gramophone or, rather, the Victrola, as it was called. The recording companies in the U.S. cottoned on fast to the fact that there was an immigrant market to be exploited and wasted no time in signing up "ethnic" musicians. Irish musicians had recorded earlier than this on wax cylinders, many of which made their way back to Ireland, but the wax cylinders wore out eventually and the quality was much better on the 78rpm discs issued in the twenties.

In the following years hundreds of recordings of Irish traditional musicians were released and thousands of them made their way across the Atlantic. In the twenties Irish radio had begun broadcasting. One of the first acts to be featured was a traditional group called The Ballinakill Céilí Band. The process whereby music became separated from the dance had begun. It gathered momentum quickly until there was little traditional dancing going on in the country. The cultural significance of these events was momentous, though dancers and musicians were ambivalent about these developments:

> The only fault that was in the gramophone was you see – the dance! There was nice music alright in it; it was very lively very fast . . . [but] it might stop before the figure was finished . . . [and the dancers] would have to stand up on the floor. So they preferred the musicians.[15]

---

14 Ciarán Mac Mathúna, Interview, *BIABH*.
15 John Killourhy, Interview, *BIABH*.

Six

The Strain of the Dance

It would be true to say that over a period 1900 to 1950 most of the important developments in the field of Irish music that did happen took place in the USA.[1]

SEAMUS MACMATHÚNA

The years after the famine up until the late 1930s were important years for Irish traditional music, particularly for the instrumental or dance music tradition. In those years over four million people left Ireland for America; each ship carried with it a cargo of music. Irish music transplanted itself in the new country and by so doing ensured its survival as a living tradition. It renewed and changed itself in a way that affected the subsequent development of the music in both its adopted country and its country of origin.

The American-Irish tradition made two significant, life-giving contributions to Irish music. One was the collection of Irish music carried out by Captain Francis O'Neill, especially *The Dance Music of Ireland*, subtitled *1001 Gems*. The other was the 78 rpm record.

Irish Dance Music in America

By 1850 twenty-six per cent of the population of New York and twenty per cent of the population of Chicago was Irish born. By 1855 there were one and a half million Irish-born people living in America. Of the generation born in Ireland in 1831 only one in three died at home.

The Irish at this stage lived in shanty towns in poor, unsanitary, overcrowded conditions and worked in the main at menial, unskilled jobs. To ease their way in the new country they attempted to transplant the customs and traditions of the society they had been born into. Music was highly regarded in that society and became a mainstay in the lives of the first generation of Irish emigrants to America. Irish traditional musicians were typical of the first Famine emigrants. As we have seen, they came from a rural background of subsistence farming and landless labourers, and they left Ireland in equal proportion. Many of the travelling pipers and "professional" musicians lost their livelihoods after the Famine and followed their audiences out to America.

---

[1] *Treoir*, 1987, Uimh. 1.

They played at weddings, wakes and social gatherings. Some, as we have seen, made their way into music hall and variety, then beginning to cater for an exclusively immigrant audience. Irish music was added to the ethnic melting pot and eventually made up a part of an identifiably American form of popular entertainment, reaching its high point of expression in the musical output and public persona of George M. Cohan.

In places, the tradition remained intact. The old tunes and styles of playing were the means of collective identification for immigrant Irish communities for whom assimilation was not a priority. Life in nineteenth-century Chicago exemplifies this aspect of the Irish-American community and is embodied in the life of Captain Francis O'Neill.

O'Neill's 1001

Francis O'Neill, born in Tralibane, near Bantry in County Cork, in 1849, was a clever student and an accomplished traditional flute player. He came from an area rich in traditional music and the O'Neill family home was open to local and travelling musicians. O'Neill had a musical ear and a prodigious memory. In his recollections of this time, he boasted that he never forgot any tune or song he ever heard.

He was still a child when the parish priest of the area banned all crossroads and house dances. This had the effect of putting a stop to the playing of music altogether and may have been a factor in sixteen-year-old O'Neill's decision to leave home in 1865.

He did not go directly to America. He worked his passage on several ships, made many voyages, and was shipwrecked before ending up in San Francisco. By 1871 he was in Chicago, where he was later sworn in as a policeman, rising to become Chief of Police in 1901.

In the year of O'Neill's arrival in Chicago, the city was devastated by fire. It had broken out at a party in the house of a Mrs O'Leary where an Irish fiddle player, Pat McLoughlin, was entertaining his newly-arrived Irish cousin. The rebuilding of the city created work for thousands of Irish immigrants and also gave them a strong position in the construction industry, which they still retain.

Irish Music Club, Chicago.

O'Neill became involved in Irish musical activities in Chicago. There was a demand for traditional music at the time, and there were many house parties, sessions, and functions. There were also dance halls and saloons which featured Irish music. O'Neill often found work for traditional musicians as policemen. The Chicago police force employed a disproportionately high percentage of traditional musicians while O'Neill was their chief.

Typical of his modus operandi was the recruitment of Barney Delaney, a saloon piper, a class of musician usually disapproved of by O'Neill. He realised, however, that Delaney was an exceptional musician and persuaded him to join the force. O'Neill had an active association with traditional musicians through the Chicago Irish Music Club, at informal house sessions and with celebrated professional Irish musicians like Patsy Touhey, who passed through the city. In 1901 he was elected president of this organisation, an indication of his status amongst the community of players in the city.

He appreciated the high quality of the music being played in America and set about collecting tunes with the help of a musician friend, James O'Neill. A sergeant on the force, James O'Neill was a fiddle player who was musically literate, unlike Captain O'Neill. Initially, the Captain made the twenty-mile journey to Sergeant O'Neill's house and simply played everything he could remember. The Sergeant then transcribed the tune in staff notation. Gradually other musicians became involved and their tunes were included in the collection. At this stage there was no intention to publish. The objective was to preserve the music being collected.

The collection also included tunes and airs selected from old manuscripts and printed sources which were considered worthy of note. A vast amount of material – nearly two thousand pieces – was notated and the decision was then taken to publish. 1,850 pieces were presented for publication in 1903 under the title *The Music of Ireland*. Hundreds of dance tunes which had never been seen in print before appeared in this book, as well as around a hundred song airs which had not previously been collected.

O'Neill decided to publish some settings of airs which had come from other collections, notably those of Edward Bunting and George Petrie. Bunting and Petrie had made their collections from the late eighteenth to the mid-nineteenth centuries. Neither had a background in traditional music as O'Neill had, nor were they traditional musicians. These collections were the work of antiquarians as much as anything else and had been presented to an educated and literate middle-class audience. Of collectors like Bunting and Petrie, Irish collector Breandán Breathnach said:

> They deserved to be honoured and remembered for their labours but their work might remain undisturbed on library shelves without any harm being done thereby to the living tradition.[2]

The publication of O'Neill's *Music of Ireland* marked the first collection made by a practitioner for the use and interest of other practitioners. This achievement ensured that dance music was preserved and remained within the living tradition.

In 1907 O'Neill published another volume entitled *The Dance Music of Ireland*, subtitled *1001 Gems*. This book has been known ever since as *O'Neill's 1001*, containing, as it does, exactly that number of dance tunes.

The first book had been criticised on the grounds that O'Neill had "lifted" tunes found in other collections and had included non-traditional material, such as Moore's melodies and airs in an Irish style by contemporary composers. In this second volume he excluded everything except dance tunes. Amongst players the book was very well received and O'Neill was praised for the quality of the tune settings and selections.

Dance Music of Ireland is still used by traditional musicians. Until recently it was common for musicians to refer to "The Book" as the source for tunes which they were including in their performance. O'Neill's book was also a landmark in that it marked an important early stage in the standardisation of Irish traditional music. O'Neill collected tunes from immigrant Irish musicians who came from every part of Ireland. No one complete regional style could therefore be represented. There is a preponderance of reels (350), for example, which did not reflect the situation in every district, where jigs, slides, or polkas might have been more popular. The collection is an amalgam of all Irish dance music and what it provided then was the basis for a national repertoire as opposed to a plethora of

---

[2] Breandán Breathnach, *The Use of Notation in the Transmission of Irish Folk Music* (UCC, 1986), p. 2.

regional ones. "The Book" went to Ireland and was used by traditional players. Inevitably it made inroads on the local repertoire and regional diversity lost out in the process.

However, it is important to understand that traditional musicians do not use O'Neill's collection in the way a classical musician would play directly from a score. The notated music operates as the outline or melody line of the tune, which is identified by key signature as a jig, reel, hornpipe or other kind of piece. Most of the O'Neill tunes were notated from the playing, humming, or lilting of a musician, but the annotated version gives no indication of the ornamentation employed by the performer. The grace notes, rolls, slides, etc., are left for the musician in performance to fill in. In a later book, *Waifs and Strays of Gaelic Melody*, O'Neill pointed out that:

> to illustrate the wealth of graces, turns and trills, which adorn the performance of capable Irish pipers and fiddlers, skilful both in execution and improvisation, is beyond the scope of musical notation.[3]

Even if it were within the scope of notation to do such a thing, it would undermine the whole basis of traditional playing, which relies on the skill and imagination of the individual performer who is free to improvise and ornament a tune.

Sergeant O'Neill, in making his transcriptions, had sometimes altered tunes to fit in with the classical scale system in which he had been trained. It might be asked, of what use is O'Neill's *Dance Music of Ireland*, or any notated music for that matter, in the playing of traditional music?

> Staff notation mostly serves a two fold purpose for traditional players. It elucidates a twist or turn in a tune which his ear has failed to pick up: it recalls to memory a tune once played but now forgotten. Here the notation may be likened to a photograph – the features in both cases are instantly recalled on sight and the notation and the photograph can . . . be dispensed with. Memory takes over as the original impression reinstates itself.[4]

New tunes are also learned from staff notation by some traditional players. In this way O'Neill provided future generations of players with a treasure house of Irish dance tunes – of musical photographs. His contribution remains one of the most significant in the history of the tradition.

In recent years much scholarly work has been carried out on the O'Neill collections and on O'Neill himself. This has produced new and revised editions of the works, a biography and greater access to the music for players. One of the centrepieces of an outstanding architectural development in the Smithfield area of Dublin city is the Chief O'Neill Ceol Centre opened in 1999. This multi-media facility features an exhibition space and audio visual presentation of Irish traditional music within which all aspects of traditional music are systematically dealt with. It is a fitting, if tardy, memorial to O'Neill.

---

[3] O'Neill, *Irish Minstrels and Musicians* (Mercier Press, Cork, 1987), Preface.
[4] Breandán Breathnach, *The Use of Notation*.

O'Neill, in later life overcome by disappointment and personal family tragedies, became disillusioned about the future of Irish traditional music. He perceived a great lack of commitment towards the music on the part of Irish people in general. He left his collection of music books, recordings and personal correspondence to the University of Notre Dame at South Bend Indiana in the U.S. This archive, known as the O'Neill Irish Music Collection, is held in The Hesburgh Library of that university.

Adapting to the American Way of Life

In the Chicago of O'Neill's time there were several dance halls; dancing also took place on social occasions, such as at weddings. O'Neill was actively involved in the Chicago Irish Music Club, which was primarily an organisation of players. The provision of music for dancing was not the only item on its agenda. The members were interested in the music for itself and were happy to play for each other without the presence of dancers. Listening and dancing became two distinct aspects of participation in traditional music.

Travelling shows like Jerry Cohan's *Hibernicon* often featured an "Irish piper" who played on the stage in a concert setting. Organisations like the Gaelic League, interested in promoting Irish cultural events, mounted concerts of Irish traditional music for a seated, middle-class, Irish-American audience.

O'Neill himself made a distinction between two great pipers of the day, Barney Delaney and Patsy Touhey, proving that the dancing/listening distinction was then already well established. Barney Delaney, he declared, "has no equal as a player for dancers, both in time, swing and execution. Touhey is regarded by some as a better player – he probably is . . . but not for a dancer."

Dancing in Ireland took place on a small scale, groups of neighbours at crossroads, or in barns. A single musician was adequate to the needs of the dancers in this context. In commercial dance halls, in noisy American cities, it was important that the musician or musicians could be heard. The uilleann pipes, for example, were adapted to American conditions by two Irish pipe-makers, Billy and Charley Taylor. Their pipes were the same pitch, established as concert pitch, the key of D. The Taylors modified the bore of the chanter (the flute-like part which plays the melody) to give a much louder sound. The pipes needed to be heard from a concert platform or in a crowded dance hall.

There is an account of piper Patsy Touhey, a famous performer of that time, playing for a crowd of five hundred dancers at a Gaelic League function in 1901 in Springfield, Massachusetts. It is hard to imagine in these days of amplification how this could have been audible; today it is common practice to mike all the sounding parts of the uilleann pipes for performances to crowds much smaller than five hundred listeners, moreover, rather than dancers. Of this same event in Springfield, it was reported in the *Irish World* newspaper, most of the evening was given up to "Irish jigs, reels, hornpipes, and 'sets' as danced in Ireland".

The Gaelic League was a self-consciously Irish movement dedicated to the revival of Gaelic culture and a supporter of the Irish nationalist movement. It drew for its support on the better-off sections of immigrant society, an emerging Irish-American middle class. It was a successful organisation in this regard and large numbers attended the various functions and concerts held under its auspices. It had the whole-hearted support of musicians like Patsy Touhey and Francis O'Neill, who saw in the Gaelic League a means of keeping traditional music and culture alive in America.

The Gaelic League did have an important long-term effect on dancing, which in a way consolidated the division between it and the music. Through the organised functions of the League, a very formalised kind of group dancing emerged which was far removed from the country "set" dances of Irish social life.

The group dances of nineteenth-century Ireland were for the most part based on quadrilles. A quadrille is a figure dance of four couples; its name derives from the square made by the four couples. These dances maintained their popularity for well over a hundred years and experienced a major revival in Ireland in the eighties 1980s. Because they are truly social dances, sets can be got up with groups as small as two couples (the half set) and can be accommodated in private houses, pubs – anywhere, in fact, where there is a musician who knows how to play for dancers.

The dances organised by the Gaelic League were more formal, and took place in halls and hotels. The League devised dances where long lines of dancers, women on one side and men on the other, faced each other, and danced steps to Irish jigs, reels, and so on. Figures developed which involved skipping in and out, linking arms and other variations. Authentic group dances were introduced also in 1898 under the instructions of dancing masters. As we have seen, eventually this type of dancing came to be known as céilí dancing.

Later still, dances which were not Irish, such as the waltz, were adapted to Irish tunes and added to the repertoire. This happened first in Britain where there was a substantial Irish community, and then in America and Ireland. Old style set dancing was eventually eclipsed and partially replaced by céilí dancing.

Despite the best efforts of musicians and activists like O'Neill and the Gaelic League to keep the music alive and pure, the second generation began to lose interest. Very few of the children of the Chicago Irish Music Club members played traditional music and the society died out in the twenties.

The changes taking place in the Irish-American community in Chicago were mirrored in the other cities of east-coast America. By 1900 only thirty-three per cent of five million Irish-Americans were Irish born. The Catholic Church in Chicago, as in other cities, had always encouraged the Irish to assimilate by becoming good American citizens. Respect for authority, particularly Church authority, and the inculcation of the work ethic were high on the Church's agenda. They wanted their congregations to shed the stereotypes imposed on them by "White Anglo-Saxon Protestant" America. Father Andrew Greely, an American sociologist, wrote:

The bigotry of these crude images haunted Irish Americans for generations. Irish clergy, eager to push the acculturation of their people, refused to baptise girl children Brigid . . . because of the negative connotations the name had acquired . . . and Nora was converted into Elanor at baptism because the former was "too Irish".[5]

From 1845 the Catholic Church in America had radically reorganised itself, centralised its administration, increased the supply of Irish priests, and engaged in massive building programmes. Francis O'Neill blamed the decline of Irish music and culture on the clergy's failure to promote it: "Religious organisations, propaganda and church extension . . . monopolise the interests of our race. Every organised effort not affiliated with the church or encouraged by the clergy seems doomed."[6] He was very pessimistic about the future of Irish music in America when he wrote to a friend in Ireland in 1918:

Few of our people care a snap for Irish music. The poor scrub who graduated from the pick and shovel and the mother who toiled for many years in some Yankee kitchen will have nothing less for Katie and Gladis or Jimmy and Raymond but the very latest.[7]

Mick Moloney believed that there was a dichotomy in Irish-American views:

There was a kind of ambivalence in their attitude to their culture: on the one hand they loved the dance hall, they loved the old music and they loved being Irish. On the other hand they wanted to shed the negative images coming from an oppressed peasant culture, and embedded in the culture itself was the dance music . . . They felt proud of their culture and . . . they felt ashamed. So you found that even as the dance music was flourishing, at the same time it was going into a decline.

Ambivalence and lack of church support alone fail to account for the fall-off in interest in Irish culture. The fact was that the mobility of American life could not support a music culture which was based on continuity. The old city neighbourhoods, enclaves of the Irish, were being abandoned in favour of the suburbs.

Dance Music on Record

O'Neill was over-pessimistic, as it turned out. Even at the time he was writing, the first commercial recordings of Irish traditional music were beginning to appear. This was to give the tradition a shot in the arm in America and Ireland, thereby providing a place for it in the urbanised, industrialised world of the twentieth century.

---

[5] Preface to John and Selma Appel, *Pat-Riots to Patriots, American Irish in Caricature and Comic Art* (Michigan State University Museum, 1990).
[6] Breathnach, in O'Neill, *Irish Minstrels and Musicians* (Mercier Press, Cork, 1987), Preface.
[7] *Ibid.*

My mother owned a record store in Manhattan, and Irish people were always coming in and asking for old favourites, like "The Stack of Barley". Well she'd no records to give them because there weren't any. So she sent me up to Gaelic Park in the Bronx to find some musicians. There was always music there on Sundays. Well I found Eddie Herborn and John Whelan playing banjo and accordion, and they sounded great. So my mother went to Columbia, and they said that if she would agree to buy five hundred copies from them they would record Herborn and Whelan. She agreed and they both recorded "The Stack of Barley" and the five hundred records sold out in no time at all.[8]

This was an auspicious moment in Irish recording history. From 1916 when the Columbia company made this first recording of a popular Irish dance tune until the late thirties, thousands of recordings of Irish dance music were made.

There had been recordings of Irish music made before this, but on the Edison phonograph. This machine recorded on to wax cylinders but it was not possible to make more than one copy of the recording at a time. Patsy Touhey bought an Edison machine in about 1900 for recording, thereby bypassing the commercial recording companies. He made many recordings of his own playing which he sold by mail order. Several of these found their way to Ireland and are still in existence.

Flat-disc recordings eventually took over from the phonograph. Hundreds of duplicates could be taken from one master recording. Initially gramophone manufacturers like the Victor company were looking for a way to sell their machines. They realised that there was a huge market to be exploited in the immigrant communities. According to Mick Moloney:

they basically started what has now been called the A & R business; they would employ people in that community to record people . . . [who] would be popular enough for people to want to buy their records, and to want to buy their gramophones – so it was a circular thing.

There was a thriving Irish dance scene in the main Irish-American cities in the twenties. It was to the bands and musicians who played in the bars and dance halls that the recording companies went in search of talent. A flurry of recording activity ensued.

Two recording artists of these years between the two world wars deserve special mention. These were two fiddle players from County Sligo, Michael Coleman and James Morrison.

Coleman and Morrison, two outstanding Sligo players of this period, were born within miles of each other. Coleman, born in 1891, emigrated to America in 1914 and Morrison, born in 1893, went there in the early twenties. Their recordings set the course of Irish traditional music for the next fifty years.

---

[8] Justus O'Byrne DeWitt in Mick Moloney, "Irish Ethnic Recordings" in *Ethnic Recordings in America – A Neglected Heritage* (American Folklife Center Library of Congress, 1982), p. 90.

They played in the Sligo regional style: fast, highly ornamented, with fluid bowing. Jaunty and flamboyant, it was and remains a very attractive style of playing, and in the hands of Coleman and Morrison superseded for a period all other styles of playing. Both were virtuoso players of great technical skill. Coleman, in particular, is considered by some to be superior in the matter of "setting a tune". His recordings are still listened to and admired by traditional musicians and music lovers, as are Morrison's.

The Coleman and Morrison recordings went to Ireland in their thousands, where they had an extraordinary impact. In remote rural areas where regional styles and repertoires dominated, it became almost imperative to play in the Sligo style as exemplified by Morrison and Coleman. This involved not only playing like them, i.e. imitating their technique and ornamentation, but also playing their repertoire. As a result, local styles of playing, tunes and tune settings went out of fashion.

Reels predominated over jigs and hornpipes. Slides, polkas, mazurkas, schottisches and highlands got little, if any, airing. The movement towards standardisation had started with O'Neill's *Dance Music of Ireland*. The emulation of Coleman and Morrison consolidated this. In Ireland and America versions and settings of tunes were played in the order selected by Coleman and Morrison on the original recordings: "Even yet," wrote the musician Seamus MacMathúna:

> more than (fifty) years after Coleman's death . . . one seldom hears "Bonny Kate" without "Jenny's Chickens". "Tarbolton" is inevitably followed by "The Longford Collector" and "The Sailor's Bonnet". Compare any old recording of either of these two players with recent recordings of traditional music and this will be borne out.[9]

Musicians were now learning tunes and techniques from records, as well as from players, and this practice has persisted. Non-players now had gramophone recordings of musicians who had achieved standards of excellence which local musicians could not match. Irish traditional music became a performance art, to be listened to on record or in concert. There are many accounts of the excitement with which a new batch of records from America was greeted. Frankie Gavin, fiddle-player with De Dannan, acknowledges the influence on his playing of these recordings. His father, who "played a bit on the fiddle", was also very impressed: "Religiously every Saturday he went into Galway when he was a younger chap, on his bike, and his mother gave him the price of a 78 . . . he . . . had a huge collection . . . Coleman was my father's favourite."

James Morrison is Gavin's favourite and, as he says himself, "the approach he had to fiddle playing and the approach he had to any tune he touched just . . . can't be beaten . . . nobody can play like that today. I work towards trying to recreate that in my own playing". Gavin is a virtuoso player in his own right, yet Morrison, dead for more than fifty years, is to him the consummate fiddle player. This

---

[9] Seamus MacMathúna, "Coleman, Morrison and Killoran", *Treoir*, 1987, Uimh. 1.

is a measure of his achievement. There are others who hold Coleman in equal regard. Seamus MacMathúna recalls the effect Coleman's playing had on an Irish "exile" in New York in the thirties, who "wept with sheer joy on hearing Coleman playing 'Lord McDonald': 'It cannot be, it cannot be,' he repeated, 'no earthly man could make music like that.'"[10]

The effect of these recordings of Coleman, Morrison and others was to popularise Irish traditional music in Ireland where it had gone into a decline (for reasons outlined in Chapter 5). Moreover, they set high standards for aspiring traditional players. They also revived respect for traditional music in areas where it had died out. It was a source of some pride that a musical form associated with poverty and peasant culture had attained such acclaim. Irish traditional music undoubtedly benefited from this.

There were some negative effects, too. The universal adoption of the Sligo style and repertoire, as exemplified by Coleman and Morrison and other players recording in America, eclipsed regional styles and tunes which made for diversity and variety in the tradition. Some, not all, of this diversity was lost out to the standardisation imposed by American recordings. Some areas, because of their remoteness, relative inaccessibility and strong music culture (Sliabh Luachra and Donegal are good examples), were able resist the homogenisation imposed by the influence of recorded music and kept their musical identity in so doing.

Today the wheel has come full circle and musicians like Mairéad Ní Mhaonaigh from Donegal are looking to their native regional styles as a source: "we rooted down . . . and went for the very old tunes and what the local men were playing."

Mairéad and the band Altan, of which she is a member, recorded for *Bringing It All Back Home* two highlands followed by two reels. All the tunes originate in Donegal except for one highland, "Neil Gow's", which is a seventeenth-century import from Scotland.

Altan do not recreate the old Donegal style; they reinterpret it, using the tunes and techniques associated with it. They are a contemporary traditional band, playing in an ensemble style and incorporating instruments like the guitar, which is a very recent addition to Irish music. They would acknowledge many influences on their style of playing, but the traditional music of Donegal is their bedrock.

[10] *Ibid.*

As the pressure to homogenise increased in every aspect of life from agriculture to food production, language and popular culture, the interest in regional music styles amongst players intensified. Because of this development it became possible for regional styles to flourish at a geographical distance from their source. Players not coming from an area with a strong regional music profile like Donegal, Cork/Kerry or Clare could choose to acquire a regional style. Today, Cork city-based bands like The Four Star Trio or Any Old Time and players like Johnny MacCarthy, Matt Cranitch and Seamus Creagh choose consciously to play in the manner of the nearest geographical region to the city, which is the Sliabh Luachra style. Sliabh Luachra originally described an area on the Cork/Kerry border but, as the style increased in popularity, the musical map expanded to take in a greater swathe of both counties and parts of adjoining west Limerick.

Individual players may choose style on the basis of personal taste, because of an influential teacher, the musical company they keep, or for what could be described as spiritual reasons. These styles, after all, are strongly rooted, crafted by generations of living musicians deeply attached to community and landscape, and are heavily encoded with a sense of place and identity. They make connections deep in the psyche both with players and listeners.

Seven

Seán Ó Riada

It's not often that a single person, however gifted, can alter the character
of a nation's culture. Ó Riada managed to do this.[1]

Ó Riada and Irish Traditional Music

The great age of American recording of Irish music ended in the late 1930s. The next significant development in Irish traditional music occurred in Ireland. One man in particular, Seán Ó Riada, responded to the challenge presented to Irish music by the twentieth century. A composer trained in the art-music of Europe who immersed himself in the oral music tradition of Ireland, he was well equipped to act as cultural mediator in a rapidly modernising Ireland.

He was exercised all his life by the question of Irish cultural identity and was particularly, though not exclusively, concerned with cultural expression through music. He was interested in developing a music which could express itself in orchestral settings, film programme music, and liturgical and choral singing.

Traditional music changed radically and became accessible to a modern Irish audience largely under his visionary direction. It was through traditional music that the cultural life of Ireland would be invigorated. The consequences of Ó Riada's work were far-reaching for contemporary, classical, folk and even rock music. Most Irish musicians since the sixties who have chosen to work with Irish

---

[1] Thomas Kinsella in Seán Ó Riada, *Our Musical Heritage*, Preface, p. 9.

idioms cite him as a creative source in their work; generations of Irish people regard Ó Riada as being the person who restored to them their nation's music.

Early Years

Seán Ó Riada was one generation removed from a farming background: his mother had left the countryside to become a nurse and his father a policeman. Born in 1931, he was known until his early twenties by the English version of his name, John Reidy. Both parents were musical and he was taught to play the traditional fiddle as a child.

It was apparent early on that he was musically and intellectually gifted. As a student at University College Cork, where he changed courses from classics to music, he had a wide range of cultural interests: Greek literature, French culture, modern jazz and European avant-garde music. After graduating he became assistant musical director of Radio Éireann, the national broadcasting service. A few years later, in 1955, he moved to the Abbey Theatre as musical director. (The Abbey Theatre is the national theatre of Ireland, founded in 1904 by the poet W.B. Yeats and Lady Gregory.) It was through his work with the Abbey that he came face to face with Irish traditional music again.

Required to arrange some traditional pieces for a play, he decided to augment the theatre orchestra with traditional players. The orchestral players were classically trained and he felt that for the music to be authentic it should be played in the traditional manner. This led him into the company of traditional musicians living in Dublin. Through them he came to consider the creative possibilities inherent in traditional music.

Traditional music in the 1950s in Ireland was a low profile and mostly low status cultural activity. It was confined mainly to the rural areas of the country, to Irish-language revivalist groups, or to a small coterie of traditional players living in the cities. The broad mass of the Irish public had little connection with its traditional music.

Unlike many European countries, Ireland never experienced a strong art-music movement centred around its traditional music. These movements turned the focus away from traditional music to classical. In the process, classical art-music came to be an expression of national culture. There are many examples, including Chopin in Poland, Smetana in what was then Czechoslovakia, Grieg in Norway and Sibelius in Finland.

Ó Riada had been classically trained in European art-music and was very conscious that this music was not native to Ireland. Irish musical expression was traditional. He was acutely aware that traditional music was gravely endangered and considered that its restoration lay in reintroducing it to the Irish people in a way that was meaningful. One of the challenges was to find a suitable setting in which to present the music, without compromising it.

He thought that he needed to do something dramatic to make people take notice of it. So he decided the best thing to do would be to put it in the same sort of atmosphere as classical music . . . in other words, on stage, in a concert even though it didn't suit the music itself, which he did . . . in about 1959.[2]

Concert halls and theatres were to provide a new setting. Ensemble playing was to be the form.

Ceoltóirí Chualann

Ceoltóirí Chualann was a group of traditional musicians Ó Riada gathered together who were broadly in agreement with his programme of cultural retrieval for traditional music. Initially they had come together to perform Ó Riada's musical arrangements for the Abbey Theatre's production of the play *The Honey Spike* by Bryan Mac Mahon. The players then went on to meet informally at Ó Riada's home and under his direction went on to perform and record for radio, television, film and the concert stage. Group playing in itself was not new. Céilí bands consisting of traditional players with the additional backing of piano, accordion and drums had been around for nearly thirty years. However, céilí bands were anathema to Ó Riada. To him they represented the most debased form of Irish traditional music. Ceoltóirí Chualann was to be "an ideal type of Céilí Band" or Folk Orchestra. The principle of variation would be expressed by:

> stating the basic skeleton of the tune to be played; this then would be ornamented and varied by solo instruments, or by small groups of solo instruments. The more variation the better, so long as it has roots in the tradition, and serves to extend that tradition.[3]

These ideas were worked out and articulated in a series of radio programmes Ó Riada presented in 1962, under the title "Our Musical Heritage". The traditional band Ceoltóirí Chualann became the vehicle for new musical expression.

The Ó Riada and Ceoltóirí Chualann albums are available on disc. One in particular, *Ó Riada sa Gaiety* is a classic recording of ensemble traditional music on which the force of Ó Riada's personality comes through clearly. The repertoire was Irish dance music, airs and the compositions of Carolan and the older harpers. Ceoltóirí Chualann also featured tenor Seán Ó Sé. Ó Sé's singing style and the accompaniment devised by Ó Riada gave yet another innovative dimension to the songs.

At one memorable concert, in Dublin's Gaiety Theatre in March 1969, Ó Riada introduced a new piece, a song entitled "Mná na hÉireann" ("Women of Ireland"). The music composed by Ó Riada was to accompany an eighteenth-century poem by Peadar Ó Doirnín, whose bicentenary was the occasion for the concert. (Ó Riada's music for "Mná na hÉireann" resurfaced in the eighties on a hit single released by a British group, The Christians.) This concert was a peak moment in

---

[2] Peadar Ó Riada, Interview, *BIABH*.
[3] Seán Ó Riada, *Our Musical Heritage*, p. 74.

Seán Ó Riada playing harpsichord with Ceoltóirí Chualann at the Gaiety Theatre, Dublin, in 1969.

Ó Riada's career, in the band's history and in the cultural life of the country. Those who attended the concert still recall the atmosphere of intense excitement which surrounded the event; the rapturous attention of the audience is clearly audible on the recording. The Irish people were enthusiastic participants in Ó Riada's grand cultural adventure and mourn his passing even today.

Mise Eire

In 1960 Ó Riada was commissioned to write the music for a film called *Mise Eire* (*I am Ireland*). *Mise Eire* documented through the use of archive material (some of which had never been seen before) Ireland's progress from British colony to nation state. Ó Riada used the great traditional song airs of Ireland as the basis of his programme music, which was scored for orchestra.

    The film and the music took Ireland by storm. Ireland had no established film industry at the time and *Mise Eire* and its score were a source of great pride to the Irish public. It made Ó Riada a household name and raised the status of Irish music amongst a section of society who had never taken any interest in it before.

You had, if you like . . . a sophisticated middle-class audience who would go to symphony concerts played by symphony orchestras. Now they were listening to fantastic (Irish) music played by symphony orchestras. So Ó Riada did popularise Irish traditional music in that way.[4]

These were exciting times. Peadar Ó Riada, Seán's son, recalls that his grandmother, Seán's mother, was:

Scared stiff in case it wouldn't work. The premiere was at the Cork Film Festival . . . she was invited but she refused to go, in case he'd make a bags of it! But then her impatience got the better of her and she got her hat and stick and gloves . . . and went down to Patrick Street. When she got off the bus she could hear the newspaper boys whistling the tune of *Mise Eire* so she knew it was a success. She just turned back on the next bus and came back to her husband and said, "The boy's done fine."

Mise Eire was originally conceived as the first of a trilogy of films. The second film *Saoirse?* (*Freedom?*) was made and the music scored by Ó Riada; the third was never commissioned. His last film commission in 1963 was the music for a screen adaptation of Synge's play *The Playboy of the Western World*.

The late Peggy Jordan, who organised folk and traditional concerts in Dublin at the time, remembered the excitement generated by Ó Riada's music:

The music in that [film] is beautiful; the music sold that film more than the film did . . . it put the music on another level and it excited everybody. Ó Riada meant an awful lot to me and to everybody I think because . . . his music was so uplifting.

Cúil Aodha

The next move Ó Riada made was geographical. He took his family out of Dublin to the west Cork *Gaeltacht*, or Irish-speaking area, of Cúil Aodha. His house at Galloping Green, then a small village on the edge of Dublin city, was a meeting place for traditional musicians, many of whom were Irish speakers. Ó Riada was a gifted linguist and within a short space of time he and his wife Ruth made Irish the spoken language of the family.

Around this time he also adopted the Irish version of his name, Seán Ó Riada. This more or less completed his wholly convincing reinvention of himself as a renaissance Irishman. In the person of Ó Riada was combined the visionary, the brilliant musician and the impresario: all that was necessary for the enterprise he had undertaken, in other words. He gave himself totally to the enterprise and the move to Cúil Aodha was consistent with everything he thought and did. He needed to return to the cultural origins of traditional music; he wanted to participate in that culture and he wanted to renew the music at its source.

---

[4] Ciarán MacMathúna, Interview, *BIABH*.

At one stage my father decided, when I was about six or seven years old, that he wanted to rear his family in the Gaeltacht . . . He had no job, of course, because he threw everything up at the time; just marched in one morning about eleven o'clock and said to my mother: "We're going, I can't stand the city life any more." . . . A job was advertised in University College Cork, which he got, as music lecturer, and . . . the nearest Gaeltacht was Cúil Aodha.[5]

Cúil Aodha is a small village in the mountain region of west Cork near the Kerry border. Ó Riada bought a house there on the banks of the Sulan River, a stone's throw from his own mother's birthplace. She, too, had been a musician, an accomplished fiddle and concertina player.

A further auspicious coincidence lay in the fact that, when he was a music student in University College Cork, he had produced a setting of a song from the Cúil Aodha area called "The Banks of Sulan". This setting is still in the repertoire of the National Symphony Orchestra. Peadar Ó Riada's son now lives in Cúil Aodha with his young family.

When we landed here, probably the house nearest the river was our house on the banks of Sulan; it's peculiar that we returned home, as it were, to the place where his musical [talent] came from originally.

The Second Vatican Council changed the liturgy of the Catholic Mass in 1964 and provided Ó Riada with further opportunities to extend the popularity of traditional music. Until these changes the Mass had been celebrated in Latin. The musical liturgy of the Missa Cantata and the Latin hymns had grown up around this.

In the sixties it became possible to celebrate Mass in the vernacular language. In Ireland this was English in the main, but Mass was celebrated in Irish in the Gaeltacht areas. For the first time in several hundred years the congregation played an active role in the celebration of Mass by saying prayers, and singing hymns and responses. The priest faced the congregation instead of the altar as before.

Ó Riada, for his part, composed a Mass in Irish based on the Sean Nós singing tradition. It was adopted by the Catholic Church in Ireland and even in English-speaking parishes where there was usually one Irish language Mass every Sunday.

Ó Riada composed two more Masses and greatly enjoyed teasing out the connection he perceived between Sean Nós singing and plain chant. He had many lively discussions with the Benedictine monks of Glenstal Abbey. On this issue they were not convinced, it must be said, although scholars continue to speculate on connections between the two.

Ó Riada's Mass has never been replaced in the liturgy of the Mass in Irish. It was estimated that as many as ninety-six per cent of Irish Catholics in the sixties attended Sunday Mass. By providing liturgical music of this kind, he ensured that the cadences and idioms of traditional singing would remain familiar to Irish ears.

[5] Peadar Ó Riada, Interview, *BIABH.*

Bringing It All Back Home featured a recording of the monks of Glenstal singing two Irish hymns, "An tAiséirí" and "The Darkest Midnight", with traditional singer Nóirín Ní Riain.

He also established a male voice choir in Cúil Aodha which sang, and still sings, in the church each Sunday and feast day. In addition to singing religious works, the choir had a repertoire of traditional songs. Ó Riada travelled with the singers around the country to festivals and cultural events. These proliferated in the sixties. It was a time of heightened political consciousness in the Gaeltacht. There were many organisations established to pressure the government for improved educational and social facilities and to provide better employment opportunities. Irish-language programmes on television highlighted the issues and also provided a public space for the Irish cultural activities in which Ó Riada participated. He was seen by many as a sort of cultural ambassador for the Cúil Aodha Gaeltacht and assiduously lobbied on behalf of people there. Ceoltóirí Chualann and Cór Cúil Aodha played leading roles in this renaissance and renewal of tradition. Central to it was the dynamic force of Ó Riada's personality.

By establishing the choir and basing himself in Cúil Aodha, he placed himself in a position from which he could explore and develop a dimension of the tradition which Peadar Ó Riada identifies as "the deeper thing, the spiritual thing underneath . . . that's what he wanted to research more than anything else".

Music and musical performance in places like Cúil Aodha cannot be equated with music in the concert or gig sense. A musical event, a gathering which may often take place in a pub, is usually described as a "session" (*seisiún* in Irish). There is no payment, no programme, no set starting or finishing time, no stage and no audience. "The premise of our culture," according to Peadar Ó Riada, "as a reflection in our music and poetry is that all of us must participate . . . there is no audience." This aspect of Irish cultural life is increasingly threatened by the country's tiger economy and the commercialisation of traditional music (see Chapter Twelve).

As well as throwing himself into the cultural life of Cúil Aodha and working with the tradition on the ground, Ó Riada worked hard at his new job in the music department of the university at Cork. He made a powerful impact on his students, as a teacher and also as a man of great charm, wit and personality. He brought traditional music into an atmosphere where before it had been of small importance. In the past it had been considered little more than a source of melodies for arrangements.

The uilleann piper Tomás Ó Cannainn described Ó Riada's attraction as a teacher in the preface to *Our Musical Heritage*:

Sean's study of Irish tunes having their own internal logic . . . led him . . . to encourage his final year students at University College, Cork to use this motivic method in composition. Many of us found it a stimulating experience.

Instruments and Innovation

Ó Riada's intellectual curiosity and interests stretched over the whole spectrum of Irish music. One of these interests was old Irish harp music. Here the challenge was how best to represent it in performance in the absence of old-style harps or harpers to play them. He hated the sound of the gut-strung modern harp, which he associated with a debased kind of Irish parlour music.

Ó Riada resurrected Irish harp music from the old collections and began working it into the repertoire of Ceoltóirí Chualann. His innovation here was the introduction of a harpsichord, which he played himself. He felt that the sound of this instrument was true to the spirit of Irish harping and harp music even though it was a European instrument. This was a controversial view and the harpsichord was tolerated, perhaps in some cases because it was Ó Riada who was playing it. (For more about Ó Riada and the harpsichord, see Chapter Eight).

The bodhrán was not an instrument much in evidence in traditional music in the twentieth century. Its principal association was with the "wren boys" or mummers who wore fancy dress on St Stephen's Day and went around the local parish collecting money and playing music. It is an Irish hand drum usually made of goatskin which is played with the hand or with a small wooden stick. Its appearance is that of a large tambourine and its original function seems to have been some kind of crude sieve used to separate wheat from chaff. The player balances the bodhrán on one knee, holding it upright with the left hand, while the right hand plays (reversed if the player is left-handed).

Seán Ó Riada introduced the bodhrán into Ceoltóirí Chualann. The late Bodhrán player Peadar Mercier recalled:

I think he liked the rhythm of it; he liked the compelling attraction of it and he played it with tremendous skill . . . he led the group with the bodhrán and that's the one and only time the bodhrán took pride of place over the total ensemble.

Ó Riada devoted quite a lot of attention to it in his radio series *Our Musical Heritage*:

Altogether the versatility of this instrument, the variety of timbres produced by playing on the rim or on the skin, by playing with the stick or with the hand, and the variety of pitch available, make it a most suitable instrument for accompanying Irish music, particularly in a band.[6]

The bodhrán has since become virtually indispensable to the ensemble playing of Irish music. It is at home in traditional, folk, rock 'n' roll performance, in the orchestral music of Mícheál Ó Súilleabháin, and the experimental soundscapes of the American composer John Cage.

The Irish musician Dónal Lunny, who has been interested in the rhythmic possibilities of the bodhrán for many years, explains the attraction of hand drums over drum kits for Irish music:

> Percussion in the sense of hand drums suits Irish music better than kit playing . . . somehow the running qualities of Irish tunes are best reinforced and embellished with hand drums and continuous rhythm.

Ó Riada wore many hats in his lifetime; one was that of the European art-music composer. From the late fifties to the mid-sixties he worked at classical composition, in addition to his other work. He died in 1971 at the tragically young age of forty and it is not clear what direction his life would have taken subsequently. He had by this point disbanded Ceoltóirí Chualann, having concluded that he had taken ensemble playing as far as he could. According to his son Peadar:

> He decided, though, after trying various experiments even with classical music played and arranged for this traditional group . . . that there was no further advantage in continuing along this route, as traditional music is a music of the individual.

He had worked with solo musicians for a while in 1968–69 and had continued his involvement with the choir. His funeral in Cúil Aodha was a testimony to the respect in which he was held throughout the country. Thousands poured into the little village of Cúil Aodha, far too many to be accommodated in the church.

Seán Ó Riada's Legacy

There is no doubt that Seán Ó Riada's contribution to Irish music enriched and renewed it. By the time he died it was in a healthier state than it had been for many years. His achievements were many, not least among them being the raised status traditional music now enjoyed. He also demonstrated to young people that there was in Irish music an energy and spirit that equalled anything popular contemporary music had to offer. His great respect and love for traditional music did not make him a conservative, although he well understood that conservatism had kept the tradition alive:

---

[6] Seán Ó Riada, *Our Musical Heritage*, p. 77.

You might compare the progress of tradition in Ireland to the flow of a river. Foreign bodies may fall in, or be dropped in, or thrown in, but they do not divert the course of the river, nor do they stop it flowing; it absorbs them, carrying them with it as it flows onwards. Our innate conservatism is responsible for this.[7]

Through his work with Ceoltóirí Chualann, his film scores, his playing and compositions, he demonstrated the myriad possibilities of Irish music. His ensemble model was taken up and used as the prototype of the Irish traditional band, as was his style of arranging. Groups sprang up during the late sixties as a consequence of Ó Riada's leading the way. Some of the best young Irish bands working with traditional and folk material freely experimented (too freely, some thought) with the music and with arrangements. Planxty, The Bothy Band, De Dannan, Horslips, Moving Hearts and many others owed a debt to Seán Ó Riada. These bands (of whom more is written in Chapters Eleven and Twelve) introduced Irish music to a wider international audience as well as a young Irish audience. Very often listeners and players who were influenced by these bands were drawn back to the root of the tradition, and "straight" traditional music benefited from this interest. It is remarkable, for instance, the number of young Americans, often with no Irish connections, who have fallen in love with Irish traditional music and who have achieved standards of excellence which equal those of native players.

The folk and traditional festivals of the seventies were attended by large numbers of mainland Europeans interested in learning traditional music. Ireland remained one of the few countries in Europe with a living and popular traditional music culture. Continental European folk and traditional cultures had been eroded by two World Wars, fascism and industrialisation. Meanwhile, Ireland's traditional music was moving on into the late twentieth century under full steam. Seán Ó Riada remains one of its guiding spirits.

Most of all his spirit abides in Cúil Aodha. His son, Peadar, who studied music at UCC like his father, lives and works as a musician and composer in the old family house. Under his direction the choir sings at Sunday Mass and undertakes occasional concerts. They sing the Ó Riada Masses or Peadar's music: "It isn't mine, it doesn't come from me, it comes from whatever is behind me – the culture, in other words."

Seán Ó Riada's friend, the poet Tom Kinsella, once said of him:

He reached out and swiftly captured a national audience, lifted the level of musical practice and appreciation, restored to his people an entire cultural dimension, and added no little to the gaiety of the nation.[8]

---

[7] Seán Ó Riada, *Our Musical Heritage*, p. 20.
[8] *Ibid.*, p. 12.

Eight
The Light of Other Days

---

*I don't think it's possible to blend Irish traditional music and
European art-music. You can only interface them.*

Mícheál Ó Súilleabháin

Irish Traditional Music and Classical Music

As we have seen, Ireland did not have a strong European art-music (classical) tradition. This kind of music was generally the preserve of a ruling English élite, and later of an urban middle class. Irish traditional music developed along separate lines. It was largely confined to the native Irish and its defining characteristics remained and remain unchanged; it is an orally transmitted form. European art-music, on the other hand, depends on musical notation; it is a literate form. With one exception, in the eighteenth century, there was little connection between the two.

Musical literacy has been steadily advancing in Ireland since the seventeenth century. In the past forty years the process has accelerated. One of the effects of this process is that the gap between traditional music and European art-music has narrowed.

Traditional music and musicians have begun to inhabit the western art-music arena. Traditional music has attracted the creative imaginations of musicians and composers like Seán Ó Riada in the sixties, and more recently Mícheál Ó Súilleabháin, Shaun Davey and John Cage, the avant-garde composer. Common ground is opening up between the two traditions; musical literacy or lack of it is no longer a barrier to expression.

Sean Nós Singing

One form of Irish traditional music that has elements of a classical or high-art form attaching to it is Sean Nós singing, although it has no connection with the European classical tradition. It is embedded in oral folk tradition. In Chapter One we saw how dependent Sean Nós singing is on the Irish language, and how its fortunes as an art form were affected historically by the encroachment of English as the spoken language in Ireland. Sean Nós is rooted in the Irish-speaking world and its repertoire is in that language, with a few exceptions. It did not survive the colonising effect of English, nor its transplantation in America or Britain.

The origins of Sean Nós singing are obscure but it seems probable that elements of it emerged out of the bardic poetry of the Middle Ages. Bards and musicians had been members of the great households of the old aristocracy which went into terminal decline after the Battle of Kinsale in 1610. The poet was the principal figure in the musical retinue of such a household. He composed poems which were performed by the bard to the accompaniment of the harp. The two roles eventually merged and the later poets were also harpers. The poems were chanted or sung, rather than recited.

As there was no written music at this time, we have no idea what the poetry or accompaniment sounded like. Once the old order collapsed, the poets/harpers were redundant. The new order was English-speaking and increasingly musically literate. It made no room for an archaic form in an unknown language.

It has been postulated that remnants of the vocal tradition were then subsumed into the folk singing of the time. Seán Ó Riada concluded, for example, that the practice of variation, central to Sean Nós singing, derives in part from bardic practices. Long songs of twenty verses gave rise to variation. These variations of necessity had to be on a small scale, otherwise the structure became top-heavy. The skill of the singer, then as now, lay in the ability to make these subtle changes. This vocabulary of variation must be accessible by the listener to enable a full appreciation of the singer's skill.

Seán Ó Riada compared the "true aficionado of Seán Nós" to the Spanish aficionado of bull-fighting: "He applauds each well-made variation just as the Spaniard applauds each well-executed pass with a cape."[1]

The importance of variation in instrumental tradition is mirrored in Sean Nós singing. Much of the instrumental music, as we have seen, is dance music, so a steady rhythm or beat is necessary. This is not the case with Sean Nós. It is not toe-tapping music.

The Sean Nós singer sings at his or her own pace. The variation chosen by the singer and the metre of the lyrics will dictate the pace at which the song moves. Unlike the sung poems of the bardic order, Sean Nós singing is unaccompanied. It relies totally for its effect on the skill, technique and personality of the singer and is always a solo form. It demands of the singer "an artistic understanding beyond the demands made on the average European singer. This is because a good deal of each song is improvised and the singer must know how to improvise in the proper style".[2]

The Connemara Gaeltacht is renowned for its rich Sean Nós tradition and is one of the few places left in Ireland where Sean Nós is still part of the living tradition. Josie Sheáin Jack MacDhonnacha and Sara Grealish are acclaimed Sean Nós singers who were born in the Connemara Gaeltacht. Sarah's two sisters are also well known Sean Nós singers, as was Josie Sheáin Jack's father. Both function as teachers and transmitters of traditional singing in their areas. For Josie the songs are "more or less the same as they were two hundred years ago". New songs are added to the tradition, but

---

[1] Seán Ó Riada, *Our Musical Heritage*, p. 24.
[2] *Ibid.*, p. 23.

he favours the older ones. The contemporary Sean Nós songs are "not as rich as the older ones; the language used in them and the music are probably not as good".

There is evidence that the Sean Nós influence has spread to more contemporary musical forms. Liam Ó Maonlaí of The Hothouse Flowers has spoken of the debt he owes to Sean Nós in the development of his singing style. This sensibility, which Tony MacMahon describes as "intensely lyrical", is evident in Ó Maonlaí's approach to contemporary material. However, he has always sung "straight" Sean Nós.

The future of Sean Nós singing will depend ultimately on the survival of the Gaeltacht and Irish-speaking communities. Right now the tradition is at a critical stage in its history, although there are encouraging signs that the tradition will continue to renew itself. One sign of good health is the uptake of

Ó Maonlaí recorded a love song in the Sean Nós style for *Bringing It All Back Home*: "Iníon an Fhaoit ón Ghleann."

It will be seen in Chapter Eleven that Sinéad O'Connor, another singer more usually associated with rock music than Sean Nós, recorded "I am Stretched on your Grave", an unaccompanied song strongly influenced by this style. The original song in Irish, "Ta mé Sínte ar do Thuama", was sung for *Bringing It All Back Home* by the late Diarmuid Ó Súilleabháin, from the west Cork Gaeltacht of Cúil Aodha, an area renowned for its fine singers. Love songs such as these are the most numerous type of Irish traditional song:

"When the Irish speaker sings . . . he speaks of love, he speaks lyrically, he speaks of the now, and it's all linked to feeling and emotion . . . and a very strong sense of place."[3]

[3] Mícheál Ó Súilleabháin, Interview, *BIABH*.

Sean Nós classes, workshops and traditional singing events to the Irish-language communities within and without the Gaeltacht.

The reintroduction of the Sean Nós competition to the Oireachtas in 1939 also did much to promote the singing. This event hosts the prestigious Coirn Uí Riada competition, the high point of the Sean Nós singer's year. Broadcast live on the Irish language radio station, Raidió na Gaeltachta, the programme attracts a big listenership within the Gaeltacht area: the winner brings acclaim not only on himself or herself but also on the regional style in which he or she sings and consequently on the area itself. Most competitors and winners have come from one or other of the Gaeltachtaí but in 1996 a Dublin woman, Mairéad Ní Uistín, won the prize. This was the first time in the history of the competition that the prize was taken by a singer born outside the Gaeltacht. As it happens, Dublin city has an active Sean Nós singing community, known collectively as "Sean Nós Cois Life". This group organises an annual singing festival in the city and runs regular workshops and sessions.

Another important development for Sean Nós has been the establishment of "Ionad na nAmhrán" at the University of Limerick (UL). Literally "Song Centre", the Ionad is dedicated to the documentation, study and presentation of the Irish song tradition. Initially under the direction of Lillis Ó Laoire, a teacher at UL and fine Sean Nós singer from Donegal, the centre regularly invites Sean Nós singers to perform in concerts and to participate in workshops on campus.

The Harping Tradition

Because the ancient harp music of Ireland was not written down and because we know very little about the way in which the instrument was played, we have no clear idea of what the music sounded like. We know that the old Irish harps were metal-strung and played with the nails, but little is known of the technique. What little knowledge there is about harp music was made possible through musical literacy.

Turlough Carolan was an important figure in Irish harping. He is known as "the last of the Irish harpers", although this is not strictly true. Born in 1670 when the decline of the harping tradition was well under way, he did manage to make a living as a professional harper and enjoyed the patronage of wealthy households, in particular that of a Mrs MacDermott Roe. Carolan is important because he stands at the crossroads where ancient tradition and new European art-music met. He succeeded in straddling the old Gaelic world and the new English-speaking establishment.

Moving in Anglo-Irish circles, Carolan came into contact with the popular art music of the day, namely the works of the Italian composers Vivaldi and Corelli, whose pupil Geminiani lived in Dublin. Carolan's works reflect this Italianate influence and for this reason can be set apart from Irish harp music which preceded it. Coming from an oral tradition, and with the handicap of blindness, he mastered aspects of baroque composition.

Irish harp music was diatonic rather than chromatic. The instrument, which did not have a full chromatic scale, did not adapt easily to the chromatic music becoming increasingly popular throughout the seventeenth century. For this reason, Carolan's tunes played on modern instruments sound more baroque than traditional. On the Irish harp that Carolan played, his compositions would have retained a traditional feel:

> Though he did imitate the art music of the period in writing tunes, when it came to playing them, the nature of his instrument was such that the melodies sounded best when accompanied in the traditional harp way.[4]

Carolan differed from the harpers who preceded him in having his compositions published in his own lifetime. The eighteenth century was "the first century in which Irish music was published in any considerable quantity and it was the first century in which Irish music was published in Ireland."[5]

Irish music published in the eighteenth century did not actually represent the repertoire of traditional music of the day. As Nicholas Carolan pointed out in his paper on music publishing, "what are overwhelmingly represented in print are instrumental melodies and song airs of a type that the non-native ear found attractive".[6] Turlough Carolan's music was included in this designation.

Máire Ní Chathasaigh is an Irish harper who plays what she calls a "neo-Irish harp": "It looks like the old Irish harp but it is constructed using modern methods . . . the feature that makes it an Irish harp is its curved front fore-pillar, typical of Irish harps of earliest times." Ní Chathasaigh's accomplishments are extensive and range from occupying a pre-eminent position as an interpretative player of dance music on the harp through to teaching and scholarship. She is a virtuoso player and her innovative approach and technique have been greatly influential on a younger generation of harpers.

The next landmark in the history of harp music was the Belfast Harpers Festival of 1792. The last remaining harpers – about a dozen in all – were assembled in Belfast for the purpose of having their music transcribed and preserved. The organisers of the festival were patriotic-minded men who also represented the eighteenth-century interest in antiquities and folklore. They were concerned that

---

For *Bringing It All Back Home* Máire Ní Chathasaigh recorded a Carolan tune, "Carolan's farewell to Music". Legend has it that he composed it on his death bed:

> It's interesting from a musical point of view in that it shows no baroque influence whatever . . . it's very, very Irish in its whole style and conception and emotion. It's interesting that it should be his last composition, that he went back to his roots, so to speak, at the end.

---

[4] Gráinne Yeats, "The Rediscovery of Carolan" in *The Achievement of Seán Ó Riada* (Bernard Harris and Grattan Freyer Eds, Irish Humanities Centre and Keohanes, 1981).

[5] Nicholas Carolan, "The Most Celebrated Irish Tunes. The Publishing of Music in the Eighteenth Century", Ó Riada Memorial Lecture, No. 5 (The Irish Traditional Music Society, UCC, 1990).

[6] *Ibid.*

this music would perish with the last of these harpers, who were elderly even then. It was reported also that only one played in the old way, with long, crooked fingernails.

Edward Bunting, then a young man, was engaged to transcribe the music. He was affected so deeply by this event that he dedicated the rest of his life to the collection and transcription of traditional Irish music. He went on to publish three volumes of collections. The first, published in 1796, contained the fruits of the harping festival and other harp music he recorded "in the field". Unfortunately, Bunting was trained in the modern art-music system of major and minor scales. His transcriptions of harp compositions sometimes put them in keys which would have been impossible on the Irish harp. Nevertheless, it is still a valuable record. Without it we would have little knowledge of this music or how it was played.

Bunting's collections and the work of the collectors who followed him – Petrie and Joyce, principally – were published and presented not to traditional musicians who did not read music, but to a middle and upper-class audience who were far removed from it. This audience was interested in arrangements of Irish airs and melodies which could be adapted to the modern scale system. This arranged form of Irish music reached its high point of expression in the works of Thomas Moore in the nineteenth century.

In 1800, as the Act of Union consolidated Ireland's colonial status, the young and precociously talented Thomas Moore became an overnight success with the publication of his first book of poetry. Later in that decade came the first of ten volumes of *The Melodies*, the music soundtrack of nineteenth-century nationalist Ireland. Moore used the old airs in Bunting's collection as the basis for his own lyrics, which enjoyed tremendous popularity in the English-speaking world. He was an accomplished pianist and accompanied himself on this instrument in performances of his own works. (The nineteenth century marked the emergence of the piano as an instrument, initially to be found in the houses of the wealthy and in the context of western art-music. As the century wore on, the piano became more widely dispersed through Irish society.)

Meanwhile, "Moore's Melodies", universally popular and sung all over the English-speaking world, came to be regarded as quintessential Irish song. Moore is a contradictory figure in Irish history, but well into the twentieth century *The Melodies* survived as the mainstay of the Irish tenor repertoire and family singsongs. Gradually they and the life that supported them faded away and with them the last of Moore, once hailed as "The National Poet". Latterly Moore has come to be seen as a dilettante who peddled a false, non-threatening version of Ireland for the amusement of English aristocrats, but in his own time the Irish populace revered him as a nationalist hero and mobbed in the street. He remains central to an understanding of the cultural development of modern Ireland, which was developing two hundred years ago and was beginning to express itself culturally in English, retrieving what it could of its inaccessible Gaelic past. In Moore it found its voice.

Seán Ó Riada and Harp Music

Ó Riada, who had been trained in western art-music forms, was interested in many aspects of Irish music and performance, one of which was old Irish harping and harp music. He scoured old collections and manuscripts and made innovative arrangements of harp music for performance with his ensemble Ceoltóirí Chualann. He disliked the tone of the modern Irish harp and, in the absence of an authentic instrument, chose to use a harpsichord. The harpsichord is metal-strung like the old harps and the strings are plucked by quills. It does not have the resonance of the old harp, nor is it confined to a seven-note scale. In any event, Ó Riada was not using the harpsichord to recreate the sound of the old harp. On the contrary:

> He used the harpsichord largely as he would have used the piano, with full chords and plentiful use of modulations . . . the two-tone colour of the instrument suits traditional music very well, but it is a new sound, a new traditional instrument in its own right.[7]

The harpsichord was always a dominant element in the performances of Ceoltóirí Chualann. Ó Riada used it as a solo instrument, as continuo, and for accompaniment to singing. Towards the end of his life he made a solo album of traditional music on harpsichord. Gráinne Yeats, a harper, identified a significant change in Ó Riada's approach in this album. He had come into possession of a nineteenth-century traditional harp. Experimenting on this had brought him nearer an understanding of the technique and style of old harping. This is evident on the album called *Ó Riada's Farewell*, which was his last recording. Gráinne Yeats feels that he would have advanced further in this direction had he lived to continue his explorations.

Very few people today use the harpsichord to the extent that Ó Riada did. Harp music, though, particularly that of Carolan, has a dominant place in the repertoire of traditional and some non-traditional players. It is played on a variety of instruments from guitars to flutes, fiddles, mandolins and bouzouki. Carolan's name is known today by people who have but a nodding acquaintance with Irish music. It is surely remarkable that a music which was once accessible to none but a small ruling élite should now be so universally popular.

Mícheál Ó Súilleabháin describes Ó Riada as attempting to "breathe life" into harp music through the harpsichord. For *Bringing It All Back Home* Mícheál played on harpsichord a Carolan harp composition called "Fanny Poer". It was, he says, a favourite piece of Ó Riada's (featured on the *Ó Riada's Farewell* album). "He used to play it with certain variations in the baroque style, and I borrowed some of these and put in some of my own."

---

[7] Gráinne Yeats, "The Rediscovery of Carolan" in *The Achievement of Seán Ó Riada* (Bernard Harris and Grattan Freyer Eds, Irish Humanities Centre and Keohanes, 1981).

The rehabilitation of the old Irish harp tradition goes on. Attempts to reconstruct wire-strung Irish harps have been successful and there are harpers very interested in learning how to play them in the old style. In 1990 Mícheál Ó Súilleabháin was hopeful about the future of the Irish harp:

> Since the 1970s in particular there are waves of very young, passionate harpers around the country, and indeed outside Ireland experimenting daily with techniques . . . I think ultimately what we're all waiting for is a new generation of Irish harpers who are going somehow or other to link back into that original broken spark in the early nineteenth century; and that can only come through a new kind of creativity.

There are some striking parallels between Ó Riada and Carolan. Both had a foot in two worlds, that of an endangered traditional music culture and that of the literate art-music tradition. Each was an outstanding composer in both idioms and each brought the two worlds closer together.

Irish Traditional Music and European Art-Music

Ó Riada's film scores in the sixties had combined traditional and European art-music to new effect. According to Gerard Victory, Ó Riada's achievement was "to translate the authentic inflection to symphonic terms".

Previous arrangements of traditional music had, with some honourable exceptions, often been dull and out of sympathy with the spirit of the music. They also smacked of cultural tokenism, a gesture in the direction of the "native" culture foisted upon reluctant composers and arrangers. As in so many other things, Ó Riada started with the source music and worked out, always insisting on the primacy of the original tune. Classical conventions were not allowed to drown the traditional sound.

This is all the more noteworthy when his other compositions are taken into account. Ó Riada was a serious composer of modern European art-music and produced four significant works: "Hercules Dux Ferrariae" for string orchestra, two choral works, "Five Greek Epigrams" and "Nomos No. 2", and the "Hölderlin Songs" for voice and piano. Of "Hercules" Gerard Victory says:

> Although "Hercules" betrays little evidence of the melodic contours we associate with Irish music, it is unmistakably the work of a great Irishman and could have been written by no one else. The type of imagination which informs it with its peculiar blend of real scholarship . . . with irony even cynicism and almost perverse gaiety is unmistakably Irish.[8]

---

[8] Gerard Victory, "Ó Riada on Radio. Integrating Tradition" in *The Achievement of Seán Ó Riada*, p. 53.

Mícheál Ó Súilleabháin

Mícheál Ó Súilleabháin is now Professor of Music at the University of Limerick, where he established the Irish World Music Centre. The music department operates as a post-graduate centre for those wishing to take traditional music studies to MA and doctorate level. Graduate diplomas in related areas are also offered. While Irish traditional music is strongly represented within the research and teaching programmes, the framework is that of "world music". Before 1993, when he moved to Limerick, Ó Súilleabháin was based in the Department of Music at University College Cork where Seán Ó Riada once taught. There Ó Súilleabháin continued the work begun by Ó Riada, "interfacing" traditional and European art-music.

For the *Bringing It All Back Home* series, two of Ó Súilleabháin's works, the second movement of the "Oileán/Island" composition and "Idir Eatharu/Between Worlds", were recorded. These two works remain popular in Ó Súilleabháin's performance repertoire.

"Oileán/Island" is a work for traditional flute and chamber orchestra in three movements. For this recording the flute was played by John McCarthy, a musician from Cork, described by Ó Súilleabháin as "bi-musical". McCarthy teaches classical flute, but also plays traditional music on the wooden flute. This is an unusual combination, but neither impinges on the other. The flute part in "Oileán/Island" does not demand musical literacy and traditional musicians with no knowledge of music notation have also played the part.

"Oileán/Island" emerged from a commissioned work entitled "Concerto for Traditional Musician and String Orchestra" which Ó Súilleabháin wrote in 1979. Matt Molloy, then and now a member of The Chieftains, was invited by Ó Súilleabháin to play the part for traditional flute. This orchestral part was written to "create a fabric around Matt's playing", using music in Molloy's repertoire.

In the meantime, the three-movement piece developed into "Oileán", with a second movement consisting entirely of original music. Here the flute line is slow and moody. The atmosphere is dark, the ominous, swelling strings elaborating the sombre theme. The traditional musician is given the space to exploit the full vocabulary of ornamentation within the piece, within the structural restrictions of the bar line divisions. *Oileán* is the Irish for island and Ó Súilleabháin thought the "Oileán/Island" title evocative and multi-layered; although the work was not composed as programme music.

There is a relationship between Ireland and England, both islands, out of which such music is made possible. Ó Súilleabháin was also struck by the island images of Ireland in Seamus Heaney's trilogy of poems "Triptych" in his Fieldwork collection and in a poem of the Irish-language poet, Nuala Ní Dhomhnaill. There is a dialogue in the music between two musical forms, representing two cultures.

The second work, "Idir Eatharu/Between Worlds", reprises these dualities but in a light-hearted way. The basis of the piece is a traditional English song tune "Jockey to the Fair", which came to Irish traditional music as a single jig. The tune is a lively and exuberant dance melody. The change from jig to hornpipe adds to the feeling of gaiety, as do the traditional percussion and rhythms provided by Tommy Hayes on bodhrán and bones. The string orchestra is used to great effect to fill in the colour and tone of both pieces.

Ó Súilleabháin did not work with a full symphony orchestra until the 1990s. He considered the wooden-bodied instruments of a chamber orchestra a more organic medium for traditional music. His affinity with baroque music directed him away from "all that colour" of the full orchestra. Since then he has taken on the full orchestra, most recently for his film score "Becoming" for the re-issued '20s silent film *Irish Destiny*. However, he remains attached to the chamber orchestra and his access to the Irish Chamber Orchestra, which is based at UL, means that his compositions are most usually achieved in this format.

Shaun Davey

"All that colour" attracted composer Shaun Davey. In 1980 he composed a suite, "The Brendan Voyage", for uilleann pipes and symphony orchestra, which has since taken a place in the Irish orchestral repertoire. The work describes the voyage of an Irish saint, Brendan the Navigator, who is recorded as having sailed to America in a leather boat in the sixth century. Davey was inspired by the re-creation of that voyage undertaken by the sailor Tim Severin, who successfully established the possibility, if not probability, of such a journey.

Davey was struck by the way in which Severin's account of the contemporary voyage "describes various meeting points between mediaeval and modern culture". He was drawn to explore the common terrain on which "old and contemporary music" might meet.

"The Brendan Voyage" consists of ten parts, each of which describes an episode of the voyage and in which the pipes represent the boat. The piper who performed the part first in 1980 was Liam O'Flynn. Nothing in O'Flynn's background as a traditional musician had prepared him for performing with the wide canvas of sound produced by a full orchestra. When he became accustomed to it he found that "the sheer size of it was exhilarating". He learned to anticipate the playing of the orchestra and he also improved his music reading skills, to extend his understanding of the score. Within the melody line provided for him, he ornamented and decorated in the traditional way without interfering with the flow of the music.

Since the "Brendan Voyage" Davey and O'Flynn have worked together on other compositions involving orchestra and pipes. Today, while still operating as a solo traditional piper, his continued collaboration with Davey has seen him perform on each new Davey composition: "Granuaile" "The Relief of Derry" and "The Pilgrim". He now looks forward to every new experience of performing with orchestras.

Catherine Ennis and Liam O'Flynn

Catherine Ennis is an organist who was born and educated in England, and went on to Oxford to take a music degree. Her father was Seamus Ennis, a renowned music collector, broadcaster, great uilleann piper, and one of the most influential figures in twentieth century traditional Irish music. He married and later separated from Catherine's mother when she was four years old; it wasn't until the end of his life that she met and got to know her father. In the meantime she had become a classically trained church organist, but was captivated by her father's music when they met.

Catherine Ennis in childhood, with her father, piper Seamus Ennis.

For *Bringing It All Back Home* Ennis played one of her father's favourite pieces, "Easter Snow", with uilleann piper Liam O'Flynn. The duo have recorded together in the past; O'Flynn was taught by her father and now plays his pipes. He, too, learned "Easter Snow" from Seamus Ennis. The combination of organ and pipes is unusual. Ennis loved the effect:

"I think they sound very mystical together because the pipes sound like an extension of the organ; it's like having a stop, but a sort of human stop rather than just a series of organ pipes. It's a living sort of vibrato beautifully-ornamented stop."

Roaratorio

Traditional music has had many encounters with non-traditional music. One of the strangest has been "Roaratorio", the work of the late American composer John Cage. It is not entirely correct to describe this music as western art-music, since John Cage was an avant-garde composer who abandoned all the fundamental precepts of art-music composition.

The work is a soundscape based on *Finnegan's Wake* by James Joyce, in which traditional music, text, and tape-recordings are interwoven. The recordings are of sounds that are mentioned in the book. These are multi-tracked to give the effect of a river of sound which runs continually through the performance. Cage, meanwhile, intones "mesostics" or word formations constructed from the text of *Finnegan's Wake*.

While all this is going on, six traditional musicians perform at will, any piece of music they wish, provided their whole contribution is not longer than twenty minutes. None of the traditional performances is in any way co-ordinated. "Roaratorio" is a "sound experience" rather than a work in the orthodox way. It expresses John Cage's preoccupation with the need to break down the barriers between music and the impositions (as he saw them) placed on it by formal constructions such as harmony and metre. These, in his opinion, made music artificial and exclusive. The sounds of life and the contingency of life should be represented in music. *Finnegan's Wake*, which dispenses with formal narrative and linguistic structures, corresponded perfectly with Cage's aesthetics of music.

"Roaratorio" has not been a much-performed work. Fortunately, *Bringing It All Back Home* was able to film a performance in Huddersfield in November 1989. On this occasion the six traditional performers were Liam Ó Flynn (uilleann pipes), Paddy Glackin (fiddle), Seamus Tansey (flute), Peadar and Mel Mercier (bodhráns), and Nóirín Ní Riain (vocals). Cage himself was present and involved in the performance.

Initially the traditional musicians thought "Roaratorio" mad, hare-brained, or worse. In the end, however, they came to respect and admire Cage's vision, and all of them enjoyed the rare opportunity to play at the performance. Peadar Mercier, who has sadly since died, remarked at the time of the recording:

> At first I thought it was dreadful – utterly dreadful balderdash, but as time went on I began to listen and I gradually fell in love with the thing . . . Everyone in life has something to look forward to; their holidays or to go fishing or whatever; and what I look forward to most . . . is another Roaratorio . . . It's marvellous to think that something that to me was ugly at the outset now stands as a little joy in my life.

Degrees of Tradition

A significant development of recent years is the inclusion of traditional music as a subject on school and university curricula. Most third-level institutions, including the universities, now offer courses in traditional music to students on B.A. and B.Mus. programmes. University College Cork (UCC), under the inspirational direction of Seán Ó Riada, was first into the field and today offers a wide range of traditional music course options, with the biggest dedicated department now being located in the University of Limerick (UL).

Opportunities are increasing for traditional and "classical" music to come together and for traditional music to engage with traditional music of other ethnic cultures. This has been a significant growth area in traditional music within the third-level education sector in the last ten years.

An important breakthrough was recognition by the music department of University College Cork of the value of oral traditional music. Since 1980 musical literacy is no longer a necessary requirement for admission to the degree course and a traditional music module is required course work for all students. The UCC course is highly favoured by school leavers and the ratio of traditional to non-traditional musician currently runs at one in three. Bodhrán player and percussionist Mel Mercier now teaches in the music department in UCC, which offers traditional music courses as part of the music degree course. Traditional percussion and ethnic percussion generally are important components of the undergraduate programme and in recent years percussion only ensembles have developed under Mercier's direction. Fiddle player Liz Doherty, well known as a performer, also lectures in traditional music at UCC and is a member of the fiddle ensemble Fiddlesticks, many of whose members were or are music students in the university.

In 1990 Mícheál Ó Súilleabháin was confident and upbeat about the direction in which traditional music education was going:

> At the moment the future looks very exciting. One of the healthiest things and one of the things that many of us are happy about is that the mainstream, so-called amateur music making river of sound is still intact. There are musicians everywhere.

Nine

Home Boys Home

In order to pay the rent we did midnight folk concerts; they were about the only thing we knew, and we had invited our friends who had told us we were folk singers. We didn't know we were folk singers, we were just singing all Irish songs. They liked them.

TOM CLANCY

Folk and Traditional Influences in the Sixties

In the sixties in Ireland there was an explosion of music. Through Seán Ó Riada a revitalised traditional music was introduced to new audiences. Meanwhile in America and Britain in the late fifties a small but very active folk music movement had been centred around clubs and progressive social movements. The Weavers, Woody Guthrie, Leadbelly, and Oscar Brand in America and Ewan MacColl in Britain worked with an agenda which attempted to make folk song relevant to urban audiences.

On St Patrick's Day in 1956, three brothers from Carrick on Suir, County Tipperary, found themselves giving their first public concert of Irish folk songs in New York city. With their fourth member, Tommy Makem, The Clancy Brothers became a popular folk group in America, gaining much professional experience there. At their homecoming concerts, where they reintroduced popular folk song to the Irish public, they were hailed as conquering heroes. The Clancys were ambassadors of folk music which was finding its place in the most highly developed urban society in the world – but it was Irish folk song strongly influenced by the Clancys' American experiences, in a form that had not been heard before in Ireland. The music was rooted in an old, mainly rural tradition, yet its contemporary expression would from now on be largely urban. Its traditional expression would also find a place in the new world of the twentieth century.

American Folk

Radio and gramophone recordings changed American folk and traditional music, gradually modifying the material from its original "raw" state. Increasing use was made of instrumentation to achieve a richer, fuller sound. The use of rhythmic backing and harmonies further enhanced this effect. The music developed further and further away from its roots and displaced the kind of community or family music-making described by Jean Ritchie in her book *Singing Family of The Cumberlands* (see Chapter Two).

Almost at the same time as this was happening, traditional music enthusiasts grew concerned about the need to collect and save the store of American folk song, which was disappearing fast or being rendered unrecognisable by the recording industry. Pioneers of collecting and recording folk music "in the field" were the father and son team of John and Alan Lomax. Together they spent over fifty years at a task which yielded up a wealth of American folk song from the old English and Scots-Irish ballads of the Appalachians to the blues and spirituals of the black people of the south.

In Angola Prison, Carolina, John Lomax "discovered" one of the great black singers of the century, Huddy Ledbetter, better known as Leadbelly. Leadbelly sang in a style of blues music rooted in the African-American community of his childhood. He accompanied himself on guitar and composed his own songs. The recordings made of him by the Lomaxes made him a household name and both father and son were active in promoting him as a performing artist.

Interest in folk and traditional music had developed in urban America after

Huddy Ledbetter, better known as Leadbelly.

World War II. Folk music societies and country dance organisations were the prime vehicles for these interests, the centre for which was New York City. Jean Ritchie arrived in New York in the forties from Kentucky and found herself in demand as a singer, first at parties and later at professional concerts. She sang family material to begin with and then began to introduce songs she had composed in a folk idioms. These were a kind of updating of the old folk material offering new insights into rural life in contemporary America.

This was Ritchie's first encounter with the world of commercial music or, as she described it, "money for music". From these beginnings she went on to become a fully professional "folk singer", an occupation which would have been unimaginable to her as a young woman in rural Kentucky.

Folk and Protest

Folk music in America was originally the music of poor communities (rural and urban), of immigrants and black slaves. Folk music had always had an association with political and social agitation, and with persecution. The struggles of the American labour movement and the lives of black slaves and poor farmers are documented in thousands of folk songs. The blues and spirituals are songs which grew out of systematic social injustice.

Woody Guthrie, one of the great contemporary folk-song writers, made common cause between the black victims of social injustice and the white. "This land," he sang, "was made for you and me." He was a folk singer who travelled around America, singing his songs wherever he could find an audience, in small towns and farms, not on concert platforms. In the days before mass communication had penetrated the country he was, Emmylou Harris has said, "the evening news". In the thirties he hosted a radio show which popularised songs like "If You Ain't Got the Doh-Re-Mi" and "This Land Is My Land".

Using the melodic structures of existing folk tunes, Guthrie wrote songs which reflected the reality of life in America around him. The thirties was a time when small farmers displaced from the Oklahoma Dust Bowl were forced to work for slave wages on Californian fruit farms. It was a time when the hobo rode the freight train and was a familiar but marginalised figure in American society. Guthrie knew what he was singing about. He had been a hobo himself and had endured poverty in the mid-west farm lands. In the rich state of California he had seen poor migrants turned away at the state line and prevented from entering.

Woody Guthrie

Guthrie and Leadbelly were part of a folk music movement that had also a social and political agenda. Like people such as folk singer Pete Seeger, they believed folk song had the capacity to organise groups around issues like civil rights, job discrimination, housing, and education. In the witch-hunt atmosphere of America in the fifties they were black-listed and proscribed. The entertainment industry came in for the particular scrutiny of communist hunters.

Seeger himself was blacklisted and prevented from appearing on radio and television, unless he kept to the condition that he would perform only non-contentious material.

New Folk

Seeger had travelled the States for some years with Guthrie, learning and singing songs. A member of the Weavers folk group in the fifties, he became a well-known figure on the concert stage and later on television. With the Weavers he popularised the songs of Guthrie and Leadbelly, as well as his own. Songs like "'Turn, Turn", "We Shall Overcome", "Where Have All The Flowers Gone?" and "Kisses Sweeter than Wine" were all popular favourites and have since been covered by many artists.

Pete Seeger

Seeger believes that a good folk melody should be used more than once. "Kisses Sweeter than Wine" is a good example of an old song revitalised. The melody is that of an Irish song called "Droimeann Donn Dílis", about a cow, taken to be an allegorical reference to Ireland. "Droimeann Donn Dílis" became the comic song "Poor Drimmer" in America, and a version of it was learned by Leadbelly in the thirties. Leadbelly changed the rhythm to suit his style of singing and, as Seeger remembers, he "massacred the words, too". Seeger liked the melody and with Lee Havers of the Weavers put together his new version, "Kisses Sweeter than Wine". This was a hit in the fifties and has been covered many times since. Seeger points out the song's mixed pedigree:

> The tune originally came from Ireland. The rhythm came from Africa, and the words from a fellow in Arkansas who met a person from New England in New York City, and was told by a commercial agent: "We gotta get a new song to record!"

The Clancys in America

In 1947 Pat and Tom Clancy were forced by economic depression to leave Ireland. They went first to Canada, then to the United States. They were interested in theatre and, on their arrival in New York in 1950, began staging plays at the Cherry Lane Theatre in Greenwich Village, at that time the bohemian

The Clancy Brothers

centre of the city. It was a hang-out for artists of all kinds. There were coffee shops, theatres, studios, and venues where artists met and worked.

But by 1953 they were in difficulties: "We were doing a play, *The Wise have not Spoken*: it was a flop; and we had no money; we had to pay the rent," Pat Clancy explained. They put on midnight concerts for their friends, who were all folk singers, to make money to pay rent on the theatre. They were so successful that, after the Clancys moved from the Cherry Lane Theatre, they continued them in another theatre nearby. They sang themselves, but also engaged well-known folk singers of the time, like Oscar Brand, Pete Seeger and Jean Ritchie, as well as blues performers like Sonny Terry, Brownie McGhee and the Reverend Gary Davis. Then their younger brother Liam joined them. Liam met Tommy Makem from Keady in County Armagh, the son of singer Sarah Makem who had been recorded in 1951 by Jean Ritchie, through another music collector, Diane Hamilton. The two teamed up and eventually Makem joined Pat and Tom in New York too, to make up "The Clancy Brothers and Tommy Makem" folk group.

The Clancys, more than anyone else, were surprised by this turn of events. They had not set out to be "folk singers". They had never heard the term until they went to America. As far as they were concerned, "we were just singing all Irish songs". All the same, they couldn't help but notice what was happening: "You could see the popularity of folk music was just coming in, in the Village only, of course, at that time, but you could see because the audience was getting bigger and bigger."

In 1956 the Clancys decided to record their first album on a company label set up by Pat. The album was called *Irish Songs of Rebellion* and featured songs like "The Rising of the Moon", "Kelly the Boy From Killane", and "The Croppy Boy", all well known in Ireland. This was followed shortly by another album of drinking songs called *Come Fill Your Glass with Us*. They had no idea what their next move would be, but by now the folk bandwagon was well underway. Tommy Makem remembered:

> Here we were with this vast repertoire of songs that most of the folk singers and folk people had not heard in this country, and none of the songs were learned from books, or from recordings; they were all from the oral tradition we had.

The Clancys adapted these songs for the American folk audience. They did this by incorporating choral singing and the instrumental accompaniment of guitars and banjo. They Americanised their presentation of Irish folk material. Guitars and harmony were not native to the Irish tradition. The Clancys were responding to what they saw and heard in the folk clubs of New York.

> We . . . saw people like the Weavers. I know I was extremely impressed when I arrived and saw them. Here they were doing songs, the same kind of songs I had known from home. There were four of them singing and they had a guitar and a banjo and it was wonderful music. I began thinking: "My God, wouldn't that be tremendous to sing some of our songs like that?" and we started doing them and just singing out lustily as well you could.

Seeger, who played with the Weavers, was Makem's main influence:

> The man was magical. I watched him on stage playing his banjo and the electricity just emanated out of him. He could get up and play his banjo and the entire audience were all involved in everything he was doing . . . He certainly influenced me very strongly and hundreds more like me – thousands, I'd say.

Makem introduced the five-string banjo into Irish folk music. The five-string banjo is a product of America's mixed racial history. A long-necked instrument with a gourd sound-box was thought to have come first from West Africa to the Caribbean, and from there to America with the first black slaves. In seventeenth-century plantation America it was known as the "banjar". It originally had four strings,

Tommy Makem playing an Appalachian 5-string banjo.

but a fifth short octave string was added in the early nineteenth century. This addition is ascribed to an Irish-American musician called Joe Sweeny. The fifth string is used like a drone, to sound a continuous note, not unlike the effect of the drone in Irish traditional piping. Frets were added later on, and wire strings were introduced in addition to gut. The banjo was used extensively in minstrel shows and in time became a respectable parlour instrument. The tenor or short-necked, four-string, steel-strung banjo eventually took over from the Appalachian long-necked, five-string banjo. This instrument became popular in Ireland in the twentieth century and, with the banjo-mandolin, was used in céilí bands from the thirties to play traditional music.

In America the five-string was rehabilitated by Seeger and Earl Scruggs in the forties and fifties. In introducing a five-string Appalachian banjo to the Clancy Brothers' instrumentation, Makem enhanced further the "American" effect of the repertoire. Pat Clancy recalled:

> The Irish in America never came to see our shows . . . They were used to "Danny Boy", "When Irish Eyes are Smiling", the clichéd Irish American songs, what they considered the Irish songs. When we started singing things like "Brennan on the Moor" and "Will Ye Go Lassie Go" and "The Jug of Punch", they didn't think they were Irish songs at all; in fact, a few people who came to the Blue Angel shouted up at the end of the show, "When are you going to sing an Irish song?" They didn't recognise these as being Irish.

By the fifties much of the Irish-American community had settled in the suburbs. Irish traditional music enjoyed no great popularity with Irish-Americans. Traditional music was found in little enclaves of native-born Irish immigrants in Chicago, Boston, New York and cities of the east coast. The Clancys and Makem had little contact with any of these communities. They circulated in an artistic milieu based in Greenwich Village which was regarded with suspicion (if it was known about at all) by middle America, which included Irish-America. Mick Moloney wrote of second, third and later generation Irish-Americans that they had gravitated over the years "towards a body of nostalgic sentimental song that painted a rosy, romantic scenario of a little green haven nestling in a corner of paradise". This, he speculated, was as a consequence of rejecting traditional music "that was associated with a low-status, poverty stricken peasant environment". Irish-Americans as a group were socially conservative. The beatniks of Greenwich Village and the politics of the folk movement were enough to put them off the Clancy Brothers. As far as "traditional" Irish-America went, the Clancys were not traditional musicians. According to Ciarán MacMathúna, who had recorded Irish immigrant musicians in America: "to a certain extent maybe the traditional Irish musician wouldn't have fully approved of what the Clancys were doing, and they still argue about this today." In fact, the intensity of this argument between innovation and tradition has increased in the years since the music of the Clancy Brothers first opened up the debate.

In 1961 they were an unknown Irish group playing in the Blue Angel, the biggest nightclub in New York, which was a popular haunt of talent scouts. The scout for "The Ed Sullivan Show" saw them and booked them. This was then the most popular show on American television. It had an audience of eighty million viewers and went out live on Sunday nights from eight to nine o'clock. As luck would have it, the Clancys ended up performing for eighteen minutes when the star act failed to appear. Endorsed by Ed Sullivan, they were delivered into the hands of Irish-America and became stars overnight. This was the turning point; after this appearance their career as a professional folk group was launched. Mick Moloney notes that "[t]hey were the first Irish-born entertainers since John McCormack to achieve international recognition". "It wasn't until we got the blessing of 'The Ed Sullivan Show'," says Liam, "that we were considered to be legitimate Irishmen."

> We were booked into the Gate of Horn Club in Chicago the week [after The Ed Sullivan Show] and we went there on the Monday . . . Tom and I were walking down the street with the Aran sweaters around our necks (now, we weren't known in Chicago – we had never been there). Some guy shouted: "Hi fellas, you were great last night!" . . . Tom turned to me and said "Hey, we're . . . famous!"

Home for a While in the Old Country

In 1962 Ciarán MacMathúna travelled to America to record Irish traditional musicians for Radio Éireann, the state broadcasting service. The musicians he found were playing in small Irish communities, in each other's houses and at competitions organised by Comhaltas Ceoltóirí Éireann, a recently founded musical organisation set up to revive the playing of traditional music. Tommy Makem remembers MacMathúna telling him that in every home he visited:

> he saw record jackets with these four fellas with white sweaters on them . . . so he took a couple back home. He started to play them on Radio Éireann. Some of the other fellas in Radio Éireann . . . started to play them and . . . songs like "The Holy Ground" just went sky high.

The Clancy Brothers' insignia were white wool (bánín) Aran sweaters. Their whistling, whooping, thigh-slapping and lusty delivery of folk songs attracted the Irish audience as no other act had ever done. Any child growing up in Ireland in the sixties knew at least one of The Clancy Brothers' songs. One of the most popular was "The Holy Ground" which was, ironically, a seafaring song said to be about a district known as the "Holy Ground" in Cobh, formerly Queenstown, County Cork: this was the port from which hundreds of thousands of Irish emigrants embarked for America.

MacMathúna went to a Clancy Brothers concert in Carnegie Hall and was impressed by the huge audience of about three thousand who attended. He introduced himself to the Clancys and suggested they go to Ireland to do some concerts. Although initially apprehensive at the prospect, they agreed. As Pat Clancy explained:

> We were nervous of it. I mean, it was alright to get up in a strange place and sing something like "O'Donnell Abú", but as far as we were concerned every child in Ireland knew "O'Donnell Abú" and we wouldn't have the neck to get up and sing it in Ireland.

Their first and subsequent Irish tours sold out and the Clancys were treated as superstars everywhere they went. Their albums were in most Irish homes and their songs were added to the repertoires of Irish singers, amateur and professional. Part of the attraction of the songs was the lively way they were presented. They were easy to sing and they were Irish, or considered to be Irish.

The Clancy format was universally copied. "Ballad groups" proliferated, as did the phenomena known as "singing pubs", offering their own brand of Clancy pastiche. Many of these groups and venues were cheap imitations of the real thing, and by the end of the decade the golden goose that was the ballad boom had been all but strangled. Singers of this type were getting a bad press, and fewer gigs. The scene moved on.

Nonetheless, The Clancys had played a very important part consolidating the folk music revival and their influence had consequences far into the future. As Ciarán MacMathúna put it:

> Somebody wrote about "Moore's Melodies" . . . that Mr Moore had taken the wild harp of Éireann and turned it into a musical snuff box. Well, the Clancys took it out of the snuff box and put it into a pint glass . . . that had more guts and less sentiment.

Ireland suffered a long and pronounced economic and social decline in the 1940s and fifties. The ceaseless emigration of the fifties had literally drained the country of its youth.

> The Clancy Brothers came back wearing, on the front of their records, dress suits. They were coming out of Carnegie Hall with dress suits and an Aran jersey over their arm. It was terrific, you know. The Irish had arrived in some way. It also coincided with John Kennedy being made President, the first Catholic person to become President . . . the energy they got in the new world – that New World energy – came back to Ireland and resuscitated people in Ireland as well.[1]

In some quarters The Clancys were seen to be playing fast and loose with the tradition, but Pat Clancy was defiant about the group's approach:

> There was always this thing: "Are you destroying Irish folk music?" . . . What we did with the songs is what's been done over generations, you adapt them to your own. The folk singers who picked them up in the cottages and the fields – they changed them to suit themselves . . . we weren't answerable to anybody, in fact we were out making a living at something we love doing, and we never had to answer, and never will answer to anybody for it.

Seán Ó Riada set out to reclaim the instrumental tradition and present it to a new, increasingly urbanised Irish audience. Irish culture was now seen as a proud badge of national identity, if not *the*

---

[1] David Hammond, Interview, *BIABH.*

Bob Dylan in London, 1967.

badge, so The Clancys were very much riding a wave of high national self-esteem. Moreover, as Ciarán MacMathúna pointed out:

> a very much wider audience than Irish music ever had before went back then to hear the real tradition; they discovered the original thing; they were led back . . . to the source of these songs . . . by The Clancy Brothers and it also brought them back to instrumental music.

Bob Dylan and The Clancy Brothers

By the 1960s the folk revival in America had attracted the popular support of a large, young audience. Many factors coincided to produce an extraordinary outpouring of traditional and folk-influenced material, as well as recordings and performances of "straight" traditional music. Greenwich Village in New York City remained the focal point of much of the new wave of folk. Clubs and coffee-houses were popular venues for folk music of all kinds, especially on college campuses. In loosely organised folk sessions the aspiring performer or singer-songwriter got a hearing. Straight blues, traditional and folk music, and contemporary acoustic song mingled. Seeger and Guthrie were the main influences and Bob Dylan was the archetype, having left his home in Hibbing for Greenwich Village and a career as a travelling singer-songwriter like these predecessors.

Dylan frequented clubs and coffee-houses in the Village where The Clancys performed, and today acknowledges the influence of Liam Clancy on his ballad style. Dylan's most famous borrowing from The Clancys was the melody from the Irish song "The Patriot Game", written by the Irish songwriter Dominic Behan, brother of the writer Brendan Behan. The melody is that of the Apppalachian folk song "The Nightingale". Behan's "The Patriot Game" recounts the tale an IRA volunteer, O'Hanlon. To this melody Dylan set the savage lyrics of "With God on our Side", his indictment of American, so-called Christian values. This song featured on the Neville Brothers' 1989 album *Yellow Moon*.

For many years Dylan immersed himself folk music. He and Joan Baez, another young folk singer from Boston, were the king and queen of the sixties folk movement. Both Dylan and the folk world were unprepared for the mass adulation and the saviour-like role in which he came to be cast. The weight of the counterculture fell heavily on his shoulders. It was an impossibly restrictive situation for any creative artist and for Dylan it was intolerable. At the 1965 Newport Folk Festival he made his farewells when he introduced to a predominantly folk music audience an electric set. Seeger (one of the organisers) regarded this as an unforgivable betrayal of trust and many in the crowd felt likewise.

In fact, Dylan had brought much of what he'd learned from folk music with him, but from then on rock was to be the dominant element in his music. In the nineties, when the brouhaha had long since evaporated, he released two acoustic albums of traditional songs (*World Gone Wrong* and *True as I've Been To You*) which reached right back to the earliest days of folk and blues. In a reversal of Newport in '65, these albums were seen as indicating a significant change in direction. Both in the sixties and later in the nineties it was a matter of supreme indifference to Dylan, who shrugged off the critics and analysts. "It's all music," he said, "nothing more, nothing less."

Continuing the Tradition

Dylan left folk behind, but others discovered the traditional source. Some musicians and singers looked to the native American tradition. Some looked outside America to the Irish tradition. Amongst the young Irish-American generation, the revival of interest in folk music gave additional encouragement to take up traditional music. Comhaltas Ceoltóirí Éireann (in English, The Musicians' Association of Ireland) had been set up in the fifties to promote the playing of Irish traditional music. Branches were set up in the U.S. and *Fleadhanna Cheoil* (competitions) were organised to give American players a focus for their activities. The competitive element has been a strong feature of traditional music in America since then. The work of Comhaltas was assisted, both in Ireland and America, by the folk boom led by the Clancys and the innovative work done by Ó Riada in traditional music. There were enough traditional players now active in America to ensure that the process of transmission was secure for some generations.

Robbie O'Connell, Mick Moloney, and Jimmy Keane recorded a selection of tunes known as "Reevy's" for *Bringing It All Back Home*. They are named after the musician who composed them, Irish-born Ed Reevy, who died in America in 1989. Mick Moloney considered Reevy to be "one of the greatest composers of Irish music this century . . . and certainly the most prolific". He was born in 1899 in County Cavan and went to America when he was a boy. He was an accomplished fiddle player, but also a composer of tunes in the traditional idiom. Reevy did not make a professional career of traditional music but played constantly, particularly in the heyday of the music in America, in the twenties and thirties. He turned to composition in the forties and his tunes travelled back to Ireland in the hands of returning musicians. From there they found their way into the repertoires of players who were often unaware that their composer was alive and living in America.

Mick Moloney remembers learning "Reevy tunes" in the sixties in Ireland and making the assumption that they had always been there.

Suddenly in Ed Reevy's own lifetime his music composed here in Philadelphia had become part of the repository of traditional music, carrying on a great tradition of composing and assimilation of the dance music in the culture . . . It's an amazing story of how music composed here in this country should go back to the home country and influence that culture itself.

Mick Moloney, who works as a musician, music teacher and academic in the U.S., has identified three types of traditional players in America. These are, first, the native-born Irish; secondly, Americans who have no connection with Ireland; and, thirdly, young Irish-Americans, often the children or grandchildren of Irish immigrants. This last group is by far the largest.

Eileen Ivers was a fiddle player with the all-woman group of Irish-American traditional players called Cherish the Ladies, named after a well-known jig tune. She went on to become a featured instrumentalist with the "Riverdance" show and subsequently a solo recording artist in her own right. Hers is a background typical of the other band members. Ivers' parents are both Irish-born, but she grew up in New York in an Irish neighbourhood in the Bronx. She is a solo performer who moves easily from playing electric fiddle to traditional music. She was taught the fiddle by a famous traditional player and

teacher, Martin Mulvihill. He ran a school in the Bronx where other Irish-American children learned to play. The competitive side to playing was actively encouraged. Winners in the American Fleadhanna go on to Ireland to compete in the Fleadhanna there, the ultimate prize being an All Ireland trophy. At twenty-five Ivers had won the All Ireland Fiddle Championship seven times. She had won the All Ireland Senior Fiddle Championship once, the third American then ever to do so.

Schools like the one Ivers attended in the Bronx play an important part in the transmission of traditional music. The breakdown of the old Irish city neighbourhoods and customs such as house dances brought other systems into being, though oral transmission is still central to the passing on of the tradition. Players learn from other players; classes are just one element of the process. Tunes are learned also from records and passed on by recordings, once on reel-to-reel, then cassette, and now on all the formats offered by many new technologies. According to Mick Moloney:

the cassette recorder . . . revolutionised the process of acquiring repertoire and styles . . .
more than any other technological phenomenon . . . One consequence has been that the
average Irish musician now has a repertoire that older musicians consider massive.[2]

This new generation of traditional players in America can and do visit Ireland frequently, unlike earlier
immigrants. For much of the eighties and nineties their numbers in America were constantly swelled by
newly arrived, young Irish emigrants when yet again the young population of Ireland was depleted by
massive emigration. It may be the case that the future of the tradition will again be entrusted to the
players of Irish music in America.

---

[2] Mick Moloney, "Irish Ethnic Recordings" in *Ethnic Recordings in America – A Neglected Heritage* (Library of
Congress, Washington, 1982).

Ten

Across the Water: the Irish in Britain

I was just about nineteen when I landed on their shore
With my eyes big as headlights,
Like the thousands and thousands who came before,
I was going to be something.
PAUL BRADY, "Nothing but the Same Old Story"

There is a substantial Irish community in Britain, one which identifies collectively with Ireland. Within this community, Irish social customs and culture, particularly Irish traditional music, persist. It was here in the Irish communities of the main British cities that the playing and teaching of traditional music was kept alive. Out of this community came a body of song which documented the lives of the working Irish.

The folk revival of the sixties focused attention on the music of this community and for the first time Irish traditional music made an impact outside the Irish enclave. Later still, in the eighties, second-generation Irish in Britain discovered in the Irish identity of their parents a rich cultural resource.

Early Days

By the eighteenth century, small but distinct Irish enclaves had established themselves in many British cities. The famine years of 1845–1851 saw a huge increase in emigration to Britain and by 1861 there were 806,000 Irish people in the country. The cities of Scotland and the north of England were centres of densest concentration. At this time, between eighteen and twenty-two per cent of the populations of Glasgow, Liverpool, and Dundee were Irish; in Salford and Manchester it was thirteen per cent.

These Irish did not assimilate easily. Many of the problems that assailed famine emigrants to America confronted Irish immigrants in Britain. They were impoverished, unskilled and often in bad health. Their customs, language, and practice of congregating together in slums alienated them from British society.

The available employment was unskilled or semi-skilled work in construction, on the railways, or on the docks. There was factory work in the sugar and textile industry, while women worked in domestic service and laundries. Over the years the Irish entrenched themselves in these occupations and operated closed shop systems like their counterparts in America. This, and the fact that they tended to reproduce Irish systems of social organisation, consolidated the conservative nature of the Irish community. In addition, the Irish were Catholic and bore no loyalty to the country in which they had settled. Britain was seen as the instigator of emigration. Built into the Irish immigrant experience in Britain, these factors worked against integration.

Once the Irish established themselves more firmly in their communities, Irish societies and clubs sprang up. They tended to be organised along nativist lines and were a focus for collective Irish identification. Nationalist preoccupations in Ireland were mirrored in Britain, as was the revival of interest in Irish culture. At the turn of the century, organisations like the Gaelic League were associated with the Irish cultural revival. League-organised social activities like dances and musical evenings kept the connection with Ireland alive. The Gaelic League in London is credited with the introduction of céilí dancing in 1897 at an event in the Bloomsbury Hall. (This form of group dancing is described in greater detail in Chapter Five.)

The members of organisations like the Gaelic League were for the most part educated and literate. They regarded events like céilís as outlets for cultural expression otherwise unavailable to them. Middle class and white collar Irish emigrants tended to congregate around the more genteel and (self-consciously Irish) Gaelic League activities. These tended to be language and music classes, concerts and dances modelled on the Scottish League's céilí figure dances. Civil servants (like Michael Collins), professionals and priests predominated. Strongly revivalist and nationalist in nature, the League reached its peak in the early 1900s and ceased to be of much relevance after Independence but it undoubtedly had a major effect on the development of Irish step and competitive dancing. The repertory, structure and organisation of competitive Irish dancing, now a global phenomenon, owes much to the dance teachers of the London League, and step dancing and competitive dancing in London runs in an unbroken line from these early pioneers.

First to describe themselves using the term "céilí band", according to Barry Taylor, was the Tara Céilí Band, which was first established as a dance band to play at St Patrick's Day celebrations in the Sarsfield Club in Notting Hill in 1918. The club was established in 1890 and some Irish dances had been taught there by a dancing master, Padraig O'Keane. The céilí band was put together by a second-generation London-Irishman, Frank Lee. He recruited twenty musicians in all and called them the Tara Céilí Band. Two thousand people attended that night, establishing the popularity of this kind of event for a further thirty years.

Lee was indicative of the close association between cultural and political identities. His involvement with the IRA forced him to leave England a year later. He went to New York where he teamed up with the legendary Sligo fiddler, Michael Coleman. In time he returned to London where he once again directed the Tara Céilí Band.

By the thirties, commercial interests were involved in the organisation of céilí-type dances for the Irish in Britain. There was a string of Irish clubs in the main Irish centres in London, perhaps the most famous being the Garryowen in Shepherd's Bush Road. Queues formed outside the Garryowen long before the eight o'clock opening and those not admitted by ten past eight were turned away.

The Garryowen Band and all the other bands who played for these dances were made up of recently-arrived Irish traditional players, second-generation players who read music, and session men. As for the repertoire:

> the natural conservatism of the exile [and] the natural desire to be reminded of the homeland, ensured that the music purveyed in these establishments was a hybrid affair – a mixture of traditional Irish and mid-twenties . . . popular dance music.[1]

Paddy Taylor, a traditional musician who played in the Garryowen, described some of the other London musicians as emanating from the fife and drum bands of the teens and twenties.

> Each district like Wapping, round that area, they all had had their own bands – they used to have competitions and everything – and very Irish you know, my God, although they probably never saw the sky over Ireland.[2]

Irish Music in Britain after World War II

There was not much outlet, then, for the playing of "straight" traditional music. This came later, after the Second World War, when Comhaltas Ceoltóirí Éireann established branches in Britain and promoted traditional music at organised sessions, as well as classes and Fleadheanna Cheoil. Very much in the revivalist tradition of the Gaelic League, this organisation had the backing of the Irish government and was the appointed guardian of the Irish music heritage. The ad hoc pub sessions of traditional players and the bald commercialism of the dancehalls did not fit into the Comhaltas agenda for music-making. It established an administrative structure that organised classes, competitions, formal sessions and fleadhanna which fed into the same structure in Ireland. Unlike the adult activity around the pubs and dance halls, there was an emphasis on family and children in Comhaltas. These activities were the nursery for second and third generation traditional players like Kevin Burke, Kevin Taylor and the MacCarthy family.

---

1 Barry Taylor, "The Irish Ceilidh – A Break with Tradition?" (*Dal gCais*,1984).
2 Alan Ward, "Paddy Taylor – An Individual Musician", *Traditional Music,* No. 2 (1975).

The late Paddy Taylor, who became involved in Comhaltas activities early on, once recalled that it was difficult in the beginning to get sessions going in London. There were problems finding suitable venues and attracting a crowd. From the start the organisation was keen to emphasise the community aspect of Irish music.

> We didn't give a damn whether they were good, bad or indifferent. Everybody was welcome . . . so long as they [had] the inclination to play. And you always hear something in somebody's playing if you listen.

From these beginnings grew a lively traditional music scene in London and other cities with Irish communities. When emigration peaked again in the fifties, London became an increasingly popular location for Irish immigrants. Sociologist Liam Ryan cites an additional motivation for emigration in "the pull of those already away". The depressed state of rural Ireland compared unfavourably with news of large pay packets and the "crack" (*craic*) to be found in the Irish communities in England. (He offers a definition of "crack" as the "jovial company of one's own people".)

The history of traditional music in Britain, but most especially in London, since the war revolves to a great extent around a series of pubs, some famous like "The Favourite" in Holloway, "The White Hart" in Fulham, "The Devonshire" in Camden Town, and others obscure and known only to the musicians who once played there. Some, like the Devonshire, have been hosting sessions since the late forties and have seen traditional music go from being the preserve of a small group of rural immigrant labourers to the highly organised professional and semi-professional activity it is today. Socialising and drinking were synonymous for many young Irishmen in London and the pub was a recreational centre, often the only one available.

For Irish musicians, pubs were places where they could meet and play together, opportunities not available to them in their lodging houses as a rule. At the height of the fifties building programme it was said that the best traditional music was to be heard not in Ireland but in London. The great Connemara Sean Nós singer Joe Heaney lived in London before emigrating to America. The renowned uilleann piper Willie Clancy lived there, as did flute player Roger Sherlock, fiddle players Bobby Casey, Brendan McGlinchy and Mairtín Byrnes, Joe Cooley, Michael Gorman, Lucy Farr, and many others. According to Alan Ward, who has made a study of traditional music in London:

> at one time or another most of the great figures in contemporary Irish music could be heard playing regularly in Camden Town or Fulham.[3]

When these players came to the attention of collectors and revivalists like A.L. Lyoyd, Peter Kennedy of the BBC, Bill Leader of Topic Records, Ewan MacColl, and the great documentary maker Charles Parker, they appeared for the first time on radio, television and on record. They were caught up in the

---

[3] *Ibid.*

Traditional musician Bobby Casey,
originally from County Clare.

wider folk revival of the time and in this way became known to a non-Irish audience. The impact of the two was to influence the development of bands like Planxty, The Clancy Brothers and The Dubliners.

By the time Sligo flute player Roger Sherlock arrived in London in 1952 he was able to establish a band which played five nights a week. This was in the Galtymore ballroom and pub complex in Kilburn. "It still wasn't enough to make a living out of," he said. "Nothing like it." He worked by day, "six days a week [with] the pick and shovel . . . mostly roads, you know, which was hard work". The massive reconstruction programmes undertaken in post-war Britain absorbed thousands of Irish workers. Unskilled labour was what was needed; the majority of male Irish emigrants fell into this category.

Factory work was also available and for women there was domestic and hotel work. Many women took advantage of training opportunities in nursing and progressed one rung up the social ladder in the process.

For Roger Sherlock and other musicians "life was pretty hectic, because you had to be up at six in the morning, and then from the late sessions . . . sometimes we didn't get back until two or three o'clock, so you didn't have much sleep." As well as organised dances like those in the Galtymore, there were also sessions of traditional music based around pubs. Sherlock met the piper Willie Clancy from Clare at a pub session in the Black Cap in Camden Town. Musicians congregated there on Sunday mornings and evenings, and this was where they played for themselves. The late Willie Clancy, one of the master pipers of the twentieth century, had also emigrated to London in the fifties. He was later to return to live in his native town of Miltown Malby in County Clare, where he died in 1973.

For nearly thirty years now Miltown Malby has been the location of a major event in the Irish traditional music calendar, Scoil Samhraidh Willie Clancy (the Willie Clancy Summer School), popularly known as "The Willie Week". Thousands, coming from all parts of the world, attend the sessions and classes run by the school and impromptu sessions of music-making occur throughout the week.

A pupil at the Irish Centre in Camden Town, London.

Comhaltas has established branches in most cities; children are taught by older players in classes run by this and other organisations. Many of them are prepared for the annual Fleadheanna run by Comhaltas.

The high point in the competition year is the All Ireland Fleadh Cheoil. Like their American counterparts, teachers regard competitions as good motivating forces for young players. Eilish Byrne, a teacher of traditional fiddle at the Irish Centre in Camden Town and a second-generation player, exemplified a desirable progression by winning the All Britain and All Ireland competitions before taking up teaching full-time.

Pupils in the Irish Centre are taught the rudiments of staff notation but are then "weaned off it" and learn their tunes orally from their teachers. According to Siobhán O'Donnell, a young flute teacher at the Centre in 1990, children developed their own style by the age of eleven.

> They'll come out with their own ideas of tunes that we've given them, maybe not so much copying what I'm doing, but more experimenting themselves . . . basically doing the ornamentation and the more technical side of it, thinking about the tunes themselves.

The activities of Comhaltas Ceoltóirí Éireann give impetus and encouragement to the playing of traditional music in Britain. The flourishing pub sessions, classes, and concerts which were part of the traditional music scene were given added life in the sixties and seventies by the folk-music revival. The upsurge of interest in the traditional music of Britain, American folk, and blues also threw a light on Irish music. Musicians from outside the tradition would draw on an Irish traditional music source, thereby bringing it to a wider British audience.[4]

British Folk

A leading figure of the revival in Britain was Ewan MacColl (whose real name was James Miller). Of Scottish parentage, MacColl had grown up in the industrial town of Salford. He was politicised early on in life by his father who was a radical free-thinker involved in the workers' movement. His mother was a singer who knew hundreds of traditional songs and from her MacColl developed the style of the traditional ballad singer. MacColl went on to become involved in running folk clubs in London. These clubs, like the Scots Hoose and the Singers Club, were based around London's bohemian Soho district.

MacColl was an accomplished singer and songwriter as well as a playwright and polemicist. He believed that folk song was a powerful educational medium, a social catalyst and expression of working-class solidarity. He also passionately believed that popular song should reflect social reality and thereby become "real folk" song. His own songs exemplified this. They took their form from the ballad tradition and their subjects from the lives of ordinary people, working people and travelling people.

His pioneering work in radio with traditional music brought him into contact with traditional singers and musicians all over Britain and Ireland. He was involved in another series of programmes called *Radio Ballads*. These were programmes recorded "in the field" which incorporated recordings of traditional music and new songs composed by MacColl himself. These radio ballads were thematic in structure and dealt with topics like seafaring, travelling people, and so on. Out of this work came some of MacColl's best songs: "The Travelling People", "The Shoals of Herring", "Dirty Old Town" and "Tunnel Tigers". All of these songs became folk standards. "The Shoals of Herring" was a popular number in The Clancy Brothers' repertoire. MacColl was reported to be delighted when he heard this song referred to as "The Shores of Erin" by an Irish singer. He felt then that it had achieved true folk anonymity.

MacColl was enormously important as a source of songs for young folk singers. Luke Kelly of The Dubliners spent his early singing career in England learning from MacColl, as did singer Christy Moore. His songs remain in the folk repertoire. Many of them have achieved the status of folk classics, like "Dirty Old Town", recorded by The Pogues, and the uncharacteristic love song "The First Time Ever I Saw Your Face", which was a hit for Roberta Flack.

---

[4] *Ibid.*

Ewan McColl in London, 1965.

In MacColl's wake came a host of singers and groups interested in both the pure tradition and in contemporary folk. For the first time Irish traditional musicians began to be heeded by folk enthusiasts, who now frequented pubs like "The White Hart" in Fulham where "pure" traditional music was played.

The other big early folk movement was skiffle. Its principal exponent was Lonnie Donegan, who had a huge hit with a Leadbelly song "The Rock Island Line" in 1956. Over one million copies were sold. It was the first British single to make the U.S. Top Ten. The result was a skiffle craze in England, which even claimed John Lennon and Paul McCartney: their first band, The Quarrymen, was a skiffle band. Donegan went on to record and popularise Woody Guthrie's repertoire in Britain and in this way introduced American traditional and contemporary folk music to a British (and Irish) audience.

Singer-songwriter Richard Thompson recalled the atmosphere of this time as being one of limitless possibilities:

> We played everything. There was a lot of work around so we tried to cover all possible bases, so if someone wanted a blues band we could be a blues band, if they wanted a jug band we could be a jug band, we could be a folk group, we could do anything really. It was exciting, good training.

Folk and traditional music combined in Thompson's later work with the band Fairport Convention. Fairport was regarded as ground-breaking in the sixties and early seventies. Its highly original music was an imaginative amalgam of rock and folk involving innovative arrangements and instrumentation. Other bands and musicians had attempted similar fusion but in Fairport the combination of traditional and contemporary material was more completely realised than anything yet attempted. Eventually Thompson moved away from traditional material, but his songs remained heavily influenced by traditional balladry.

The Same Old Story

Paul Brady was twenty-two years old when he arrived in London, as a professional musician with folk group The Johnstons. With Irish chart success behind them, The Johnstons decided to base themselves in England to take advantage of the burgeoning folk-music revival there. They had three very successful years in Britain gigging, recording and making television appearances. They performed a mixture of

The two Thompson songs recorded in Nashville for *Bringing It All Back Home* are contemporary ballads of striking melodic beauty and fine lyrical construction. Irish singer Mary Black, formerly a singer in the folk idiom, joined Thompson on both, while traditional singer Dolores Keane appears on "The Dimming of The Day".

"The Dimming of the Day" is a love song, musically and lyrically connected to traditional song. Its decorated melody line, folk-song cadences and acoustic backing do not make for easy categorising into folk or rock, which is no bad thing.

This old house is falling down around my ears
I'm drowning in the river of my tears
When all my will is done you hold me sway
I need you at the dimming of the day.

The second song, "Waltzings for Dreamers", is a straightforward country ballad in 3/4 waltz time. It demonstrates Thompson's considerable lyrical talents and mastery of the popular song form and has been much covered.

contemporary folk and traditional songs with an emphasis on well-developed instrumental arrangements. Like many other trad and folk artists of the time, they were influenced by Ewan MacColl and recorded and had a hit with his song "The Travelling People". When not travelling or gigging, Brady lived "in an Irish ghetto area of Kilburn . . . I used to associate with Irish people all the time (I didn't know any English people) who went to Irish bars and played Irish music". In so doing he was conforming to the stereotype of the newly-arrived Irishman in England. Typical, too, of the Irish who arrived in England for the first time was the tendency to come without money, job or accommodation secured. Liam Ryan has described the situation of the Irish immigrant as a problem

> compounded with sheer irresponsibility. The man who wouldn't dream of going to Dublin without a job and place to stay often stepped readily off the train at Paddington or Euston with no skills, no job, no money and nowhere to live.[5]

Brady was struck by the numbers of Irishmen who had come over years before:

> They'd go to England to make their pile and [plan to] come back home and buy the cottage in the west of Ireland . . . But they never managed to extricate themselves . . . they end up in the middle of London somewhere in pubs drinking themselves to death because they know now that they're never really going to get back . . . you knew they were never ever going to go back to Ireland . . . and that made me very sad.

Many years later, when he had returned to rock music and was writing his own material, Brady wrote a song called "Nothing but the Same Old Story" based on the collective immigrant experiences of those men he encountered in the sixties. This song quickly established itself as an anthem amongst Irish people living away from home and most Brady concerts are punctuated with requests for the song shouted from the floor. Its anthemic quality and authentic voice are recognised by audiences everywhere, but particularly by emigrants.

> *Hey Johnny can't wait until Saturday night,*
> *Got a thirst that's raging,*
> *Know a place where we can put that right*
> *Wash away the confusion,*
> *Hose down this fire inside. But look out!*
> *'Cause I'll tear you into pieces if you cross me.*

The lives of many Irish immigrants in London reflect this reality. Nor is Brady the only songwriter to document the loneliness and anger of the forgotten Irish. The statistics still show a disproportionately

---

[5] Liam Ryan, "Irish Emigration to Britain since World War II" in *The Irish at Home and Abroad* (Wolfhound Press, 1990), p. 52.

The Pogues

high propensity of Irish people in Britain admitted to mental hospitals, involved in crime, homeless and dependent on social welfare. This was the milieu in which Shane MacGowan found inspiration for his best songs, written in the seventies and eighties.

The Pogues and Shane MacGowan

Journalist Eamonn McCann, writing in *Hot Press* in 1988, defined The Pogues as "Irish music viewed through the prism of a North London sensibility". The Pogues and Shane MacGowan took traditional and folk-based Irish music and fired it in the crucible of modern Irish emigration.

They emerged in the early eighties as a band who played a chaotic set of stock Irish rebel tunes in London clubs. Their name is an abbreviation of their original name, The Pogue Mahones. Pogue mahone, or *pog mo thoin*, is a put-down in Irish, literally "kiss my arse". The name-change came about when a Gaelic-speaking television producer rumbled it. Elvis Costello remembers hearing them in the early days: "I first saw The Pogues in a . . . sort of arts club . . . They did half a dozen songs all in G at the same speed, total gala stuff; it was hard to pick up what was going on among it."

What had happened was that Irish ballads, like those popularised by the Clancys, collided with punk. The Pogues' music represented children of the sixties "born after Carlow building workers had set up homes with Mayo nurses". They were assimilated to the extent that they had been reared, educated and socialised in Britain. The anodyne and essentially sentimental ballad culture of the emigrant Irish communities repelled them, yet The Pogues were conscious that they were Irish in Britain, not fully one or the other.

The music connected to punk in its anarchic, countercultural political take on life in Thatcher's Britain. Nevertheless, The Pogues' music was culturally familiar once the packaging was stripped away. Elvis Costello describes The Pogues' music as "a promise of a good time". Off stage and on, The Pogues disported themselves like archetypal Paddies: hard drinking, bad mannered, foul mouthed and unkempt. Needless to say, The Pogues' music, attitudes and lifestyle outraged a wide range of people, from parents to traditionalists.

For Elvis Costello, The Pogues were a blast of fresh air in the stultifying environment of late seventies folk music. He observed that there were those

> who sort of resented The Pogues . . . because they've been trying to grab a bigger audience and they've been never able to succeed . . . they can't see that it's basically dead end what they're doing

as distinct from those "pure" traditional musicians who "have no truck with commercialism and don't desire greater attention [but] follow their chosen line in their own way". He engaged The Pogues as tour support with his band and later worked with them as producer in 1987 on the "The Wild Rover" single, which was more "deconstructed" than produced.

> I got what I thought was one degree of revenge in the recording . . . of The Pogues doing "The Wild Rover". Something I'd wanted to do for a long time was beat that song up. Although it has fond memories for some people . . . it was the bane of my life when I was first starting out 'cos some half wit could get up and sing that song at the end of the night and go down a storm . . . There'd be a few of us there with songs, however good they were, but at least we'd have written them ourselves.

For Christy Moore, who recorded MacGowan's "Fairytale of New York" for *Bringing It All Back Home*, "he's the one writer of all the modern writers that I can connect with . . . he just has ways of describing things that I can really relate to; he can sum up something in a way that I can understand."

Christy Moore and Dónal Lunny

Songwriter Shane MacGowan
of The Pogues.

The Pogues depended heavily on Shane MacGowan for songs, and his early promise as a songwriter has been realised.

"The Pogues", remarked Elvis Costello, "saved folk from the folkies."

Mischievous Ghost: Elvis Costello

Elvis Costello is the stage name of Declan MacManus. Costello does not identify himself as Irish, although he was born into the Irish community of Birkenhead on Merseyside. The MacManuses emigrated from "God knows where" in Ireland three generations ago. It was a musical household. Costello's grandfather trained as a musician in the British army. His father, Ross MacManus, was a professional singer with the Joe Loss Orchestra, a popular English dance band. Ross had started out as a jazz trumpet player, had wide musical tastes and as a dance-band singer performed many covers, including all the chart music of the day.

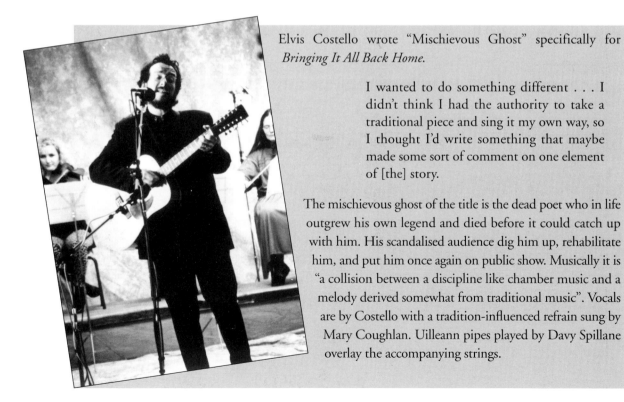

Elvis Costello wrote "Mischievous Ghost" specifically for *Bringing It All Back Home*.

> I wanted to do something different . . . I didn't think I had the authority to take a traditional piece and sing it my own way, so I thought I'd write something that maybe made some sort of comment on one element of [the] story.

The mischievous ghost of the title is the dead poet who in life outgrew his own legend and died before it could catch up with him. His scandalised audience dig him up, rehabilitate him, and put him once again on public show. Musically it is "a collision between a discipline like chamber music and a melody derived somewhat from traditional music". Vocals are by Costello with a tradition-influenced refrain sung by Mary Coughlan. Uilleann pipes played by Davy Spillane overlay the accompanying strings.

Costello grew up in London where his earliest musical influence was rock 'n' roll. Irish folk music was also played and sung around the house, but Costello came to dislike the English folk scene because of its puritanical stance. Nevertheless, his first gigs as a singer-songwriter were in folk clubs. He recalled an occasion when Ewan MacColl, in the first row of the audience, fell asleep during his set. In the post-punk era, after the Sex Pistols, Costello formed one of the most important new-wave bands of the day, The Attractions. His output of songs and albums since that time has been prolific and across many genres, from quartet music to jazz to rock 'n' roll. His album *Spike the Beloved Entertainer* featured over thirty-two musicians, including Roger McGuinn and Chrissie Hynde. Six Irish musicians worked on the album, most of them in the traditional idiom.

I started with rock 'n' roll and you don't really think of it in a scholarly way, then you start to take it apart like a child with a toy and you see that there's blues and there's country . . . Then you go back from country into American music, and you go back from American folk music and you end up in Scotland or Ireland eventually.

Eleven

Moving On

We had this idea of Ireland rammed down our throats. So we threw it up.

BONO, U2

The Rocking of Irish Music

The introduction of free post-primary education in 1964, falling emigration rates, rising standards of living, urbanisation and the arrival of television (RTÉ, the state broadcasting network, was established in 1962) all contributed to the process of modernisation in Ireland. The country entered a phase of rapid development in the sixties after decades of stagnation. Ireland entered the Common Market (subsequently the European Union) and these and other factors provided the conditions in which consumer culture could flourish. For the first time in the country's history young people emerged as an identifiable section of Irish society, with a "youth culture" in which consumerism would become more and more its defining characteristic.

Social control was a key element in the Irish state prior to the sixties and pervaded every aspect of the public and private life of the average Irish person, particularly women (contraceptives, including the Pill, were illegal). These control structures were maintained largely through the institutions of the Catholic Church and its dominant role in the education and health systems. This monolith came under sustained attack during the sixties when Ireland's growing young population presented a forceful challenge to this agenda. A booming jobs market and an affluent middle class allowed young people in Ireland a level of personal autonomy unthinkable in previous generations.

It was thus against a background of social change that British radio and television stations, American TV programmes and the international music industry grew powerful. There was a marked countercultural element to this process whereby former socially endorsed modes of behaviours and attitudes were rejected. This was the point at which native Irish music in all its forms engaged with the world of commercial music, i.e. the music industry. At a countercultural level, pop and rock music suggested possibilities of individual freedom totally at odds with the prevailing norms. This music opened up the contemporary world and expressed the reality of modern life for many young people. Significantly, it was to have long-term implications for the future of traditional music in Ireland.

Show Bands

Mainstream Irish music of the sixties expressed itself through ballad groups modelled on The Clancy Brothers and through the "show bands". Ballad singing generally took place in pubs and concert halls and was usually a singalong type of family entertainment. "Ballad session" radio and television programmes were also popular. Most families' record collection boasted a couple of ballad albums.

Show bands were primarily dance bands. Dance halls were the social centres for young Irish adults in the sixties, particularly in rural Ireland. These so-called "Ballrooms of Romance" were places where young people could enjoy a measure of unsupervised leisure time with members of the opposite sex and participate in youth culture to a small degree. Irish dance halls frequently accommodated between two and three thousand people and many show bands worked every night of the week. Show bands played only covers and original material was discouraged. The line-up was usually seven to ten musicians comprising guitars, bass, drums, vocals and a brass section. The musicians were always neatly turned out and suited alike.

Dances turned in a huge profit and offered lucrative work to musicians in the bigger bands. It was a crudely exploitative system. Show band managers operated a monopoly. Their venues were not open to groups performing other material. Music like rock 'n' roll, r'n'b or blues were excluded; the system forced musicians to work in show bands when their musical preferences lay elsewhere. Many well known Irish musicians, such as Van Morrison, the late Rory Gallagher, Arty McGlynn and Keith Donald, to name but a few, spent their early professional careers on the road with show bands until circumstances allowed them to change direction.

This situation gradually changed. Clubs opened in the cities to cater for different kinds of music. Universities and colleges around the country also provided venues for fledgling bands and provided alternatives to ballad groups and show bands.

One For the Money, Two For the Show

Singer-songwriter Paul Brady's early enthusiasms were for Elvis Presley, Chuck Berry, Jerry Lee Lewis, and Little Richard. He played the piano and greatly admired American rock 'n' roll piano players.

Coinciding with his initiation into rock 'n' roll, the Clancy Brothers were storming through Ireland. Brady remembers not being "musically disposed to that kind of thing" but being drawn in by their energy and success despite himself. He never saw The Clancy Brothers phenomenon as part of a "folk movement", though. "This was still popular culture in Ireland . . . it was just around."

This was a common feeling amongst young people. Folk songs and ballads were "just around" and not an exciting or interesting genre in themselves. Many young people who attended school in the sixties and early seventies shared the experience of Bono and Philip Chevron, who use the same expression to describe their experience of The Clancy Brothers: they were "rammed down our throats".

The ballad-group format was generally harmony singing, accompanied by indifferent guitar playing. There was no emphasis on instrumental playing and no attempt to include instrumental music. The energy and drive that characterised The Clancy Brothers was not really equalled by the copycat groups who tended to cover the same material. The ballad seam was exhausted by the late sixties and ballad groups slowly faded from the scene.

Meanwhile, American and English bands like the Byrds, The Lovin' Spoonful, The Rolling Stones, and musicians like Eric Clapton, Bob Dylan and others incorporated elements of traditional music in their performance. The black tradition of blues singing and instrumentation, white folk song, and old-time country music were surfacing in popular music. Mixed up in the cocktail of rock 'n' roll, it arrived in Ireland and met an indigenous music culture of traditional music and ballad singing. Seán Ó Riada's creative reworking of traditional music and old harp music had partly prepared the ground for the next generation of Irish musicians.

Because Ireland was a small country with a population of less than three million people, there was no great degree of specialisation in the beginning. Musicians simply took whatever they liked from the music on offer, and this eclecticism produced results of varying quality. Many musicians who played in the pubs and clubs around Dublin and elsewhere eventually wound up playing with all the other musicians on the scene. Thus, blues players mixed with traditional, folk, rock, and contemporary players.

Alec Finn, a member of the traditionally based group De Dannan, came to live in Dublin in the sixties where he shared a flat with rock musician Phil Lynott. His main interest then was in the blues, but he also listened to traditional and rock music. "It didn't matter," he says of that time, "whether you were a traditional musician or a rock musician. They all sort of drank in the same bars to a great extent and had jams together and what have you. Everyone blended in very well together."

Since the sixties the pub has become particularly significant in Irish cultural life (see Chapter 12). It was and is associated with the playing of music. It provided Finn and many others with their first introduction to Irish traditional music:

> In England when I used to play country blues, we used to look for sessions in pubs . . . although we were looked on as being a bit peculiar for doing so. But I found it amazing when I came to Ireland that people just went into pubs, [who] virtually didn't know each other, [and who] played the same kind of music and could sit down and have all this amazing interaction . . . that was the most amazing thing about it . . . I don't think it exists anywhere else in the world.

The pub was the place where many Irish musicians learned to play, where they met other musicians and heard other kinds of music. A music that was rock-inspired but Irish in character grew out of this interaction.

Horslips

Celtic Rock

Barry Devlin, Jim Lockhart, Eamonn Carr, Charles O'Connor, and Johnny Fean were young men about Dublin town in the late sixties. The band they formed, Horslips, had a name which sounded like a conflation of two Irish traditional dance forms: the hornpipe and the slip jig. They were undoubtedly an influential and tremendously popular Irish band and spawned a whole new sub-category of Irish music, namely Celtic Rock, a kind of glam rock meets small "t" traditional music.

Horslips developed a mix of country, traditional and folk rock, which was a reflection of the kind of music they were hearing in the clubs and pubs around Dublin at the time. Coincidentally, a by-product of psychedelic hippie culture was an (admittedly superficial) curiosity about ancient Celtic Ireland and this went into the mix, too. The "mythic" and portentous were important visual and conceptual elements in the band's presentation, which ran to high camp in set design, costume and thematic grandiosity.

Horslips were middle class and college educated. They worked in advertising; they were fashion conscious; they were adept manipulators of the young public's appetite for glamour and spectacle. They used their considerable skills in presenting the band in this way. They fed into the mass disaffection of young people in Ireland with "official" Irish culture as presented by the Irish tourist board, Irish radio, Irish schools, and so on. So there was an ironic aspect to the band's Celtic posturing and gender bending.

On the other hand, Horslips included members whose knowledge of Irish ranged from fluent to fair and who were interested in, and players of, Irish traditional music (although not from traditional music backgrounds). They were committed to bringing in an Irish cultural dimension and eschewed the American and British electric rock clone models. They sought a sound and material that would be clearly Irish but also successful popular music. As Jim Lockhart described it:

> It was a matter of trying to hold out for a more integrated culture as opposed to something second-hand . . . which meant forging a new idiom . . . It was an attempt to create something indigenous and new, but essentially indigenous.

Horslips' mixture of acoustic and rock interpretations of Irish instrumental music was deeply appealing to a young Irish audience. It touched a nerve of collective identity that hadn't quite been cauterised by the wholesale commercialisation of popular music.

The band's imaginative approach to set design and staging involved coloured back projections and Celtic motifs. Elements of theatricality were incorporated which echoed the avant-garde presentations of artists like David Bowie. This was the way rock, pop and ultimately all forms of popular music would be staged in the future. In a country not noted for its visual sensitivity, Horslips were cutting edge.

In 1972 they recorded their first album. In a display of their unerring sense for the appropriate cool gesture, they hired the Rolling Stones' mobile recording studio and released the album *Horslips – Happy to Meet Sorry to Part* on their own label. The thirteen tracks included traditional dance tunes and songs, two of which were in Irish. The range of instruments included electric and acoustic guitars and fiddles, bodhrán, keyboards, flute, mandolin and concertina. The record was an instant success and regarded as a musical breakthrough. Celtic Rock was born. Horslips even managed to break the show band stranglehold of the dance halls. Singles released subsequently, principally "Dearg Donn" and "King of the Fairies", classic Celtic rockers, raced to the top of the charts and stayed there.

From 1972 until their demise in 1980 Horslips recorded ten albums. They wrote their own material and used Irish dance tunes, old harp music, airs and marches, songs in Irish and English, and folk music of other cultures. Throughout the seventies they toured extensively in Ireland, Europe and the U.S. They achieved cult status in parts of America, were briefly popular in Britain during the folk rock era, but never succeeded in breaking into the international rock world. Celtic rock never did translate into the international language of rock. A millennial re-release of the Horslips material yielded sales figures which indicate that there is still a taste for this brand of Irish music. Culturally it is very time specific stuff, but nostalgia is a commodity too.

Horslips had set out to develop an indigenous rock idiom and for a while they achieved this. Singer-songwriter Philip Chevron, who was a member of The Pogues, remembered growing up in Dublin in the sixties hating ballads and Irish music generally and then being struck by the Horslips' thunderbolt:

> Irish music as officially presented didn't speak for me or for thousands upon thousands like me. But Horslips did and some Horslips fans then went away and listened to Seán Ó Riada records.[1]

Chevron himself was one of those drawn by the tradition that inspired the band. The Celtic rock craze spawned a few bands in the Horslips' mode, like Spud and Mushroom, all forgettable and none matching the ingenuity or style of the prototype. This phase in Irish music history ended with the last Horslips gigs in 1980. The band heralded the future for indigenous Irish music in one important way. It introduced the idea of bringing traditionally influenced music and contemporary theatrical presentation together. This approach to staging Irish traditional music would pick up momentum during the eighties and reached its apotheosis in the stage show spectacular "Riverdance".

Whiskey in the Jar/Irish Rock

In March 1973, a couple of months after Horslips released their first album, an Irish single went into the English charts and reached number six. The singer was Phil Lynott, an Irishman born in England of an Irish mother and Brazilian father. The band was Thin Lizzy and the song "Whiskey In The Jar" was a hackneyed staple of the ballad group repertoire with a well-known chorus:

> *Whack fol de daddy o*
> *Whack fol de daddy o*
> *There's whiskey in the jar.*

Initially Thin Lizzy had recorded the song as a jokey thrashing of The Clancy Brothers' version. Lynott was a singer and songwriter heavily influenced by Jimi Hendrix and progressive rock music of the day.

---

[1] Philip Chevron, *Hot Press*, Vol. 12, No. 6, 7 April, 1988.

Phil Lynott, who brought an Irish sensibility to rock music in the seventies.

He had also spent time with the folk and blues players around Dublin and was attracted by the lyrical element in the folk repertoire. The record company felt that "Whiskey in the Jar", originally destined to be a B-side on the new Lizzy single, would make a better A-side. They were right. The song was also a runaway success in Ireland where it received continuous airplay. From its anarchic opening guitar riff to the end, it deconstructed '60s Irish balladry in three noisy minutes.

Lynott's songwriting, however, was located in that ballad form. Contemporary Ireland, particularly in the Dublin of his childhood, featured in his songs. His skilful, lyrical evocations of life in sixties and seventies Ireland resonated with young working class fans. Early in the seventies Thin Lizzy consolidated the heavy rock dimension which had been present from the beginning and gained admission to the American and British progressive rock circuit where they achieved the status of superstars in the mid-seventies. Tragically, Lynott died at thirty-seven years of age and it fell to other bands to carry the Irish voice onto the world stage.

Caledonian Soul/Van Morrison

From the beginning, jazz, blues, gospel and traditional music combined in a way that was inimitably Van Morrison. This is still true after more than thirty years of recording, writing and playing. In the eighties his abiding preoccupation was with the Celtic roots of his musical inspiration. He is on record

Van Morrison

as saying that Celtic music, which he defines as the music of Scotland and Ireland, is "soul music". The spirit of this music has animated his work intensely over the past eight or nine years, but was apparent in some of his earlier albums also. Ireland, and the Belfast of his youth, are at the centre of his creative source, as evidenced in tracks like "Madame George" and "Cypress Avenue" on the album *Astral Weeks*. The mystical, soulful quality of his songwriting arises from his belief in a "Celtic" consciousness. Morrison uses term "Celtic" very precisely to denote the music of Ireland and Scotland and there is much to connect these two traditional cultures.

It is in his native Ulster where this connection is most evident. Unfortunately, the appropriation of the term "Celtic" mainly, but not solely, by the music industry has transposed the term into a convenient branding label (see Chapter Twelve).

In 1973 on *Hardnose the Highway* Morrison recorded the folk song "Purple Heather". Coincidentally, this was recorded nearly ten years earlier by The Clancy Brothers. In their repertoire it was popularly known as "Will Ye Go Lassie Go". It is a Scottish folk song which had been popular in Ireland for many years and Morrison picked it up in Belfast:

> I heard the McPeakes do it at a party in Belfast a long, long time ago. I'd probably heard it from my mother but the McPeakes sold me on it. I thought it was one of the greatest things I'd ever heard. Period. On record or off record.[2]

---

[2] Van Morrison to Donal Corvan, *Hot Press*, Vol. 1, No. 1, June 1977.

The McPeakes were a well-known Belfast family with a large repertoire of folk songs. Francey and Francis McPeake, father and son, were also accomplished uilleann pipers. The family had a unique style of harmony singing accompanied by uilleann pipes, not an instrument used for this purpose. In the fifties they were visited by song collectors like Peter Kennedy from BBC radio and by Pete Seeger, who filmed them in Belfast in 1953.

Morrison's nasal tonality on the vocals of "Purple Heather" and his deployment of the extended decorative melody line echoed traditional singing in style and construction. In 1980 he devoted much time to studying Celtic culture, in its philosophical and mystical dimensions. This was by way of a reaction to his early exposure to the commercial world of the music-recording industry, of which he was suspicious and about whose motivations he remains cynical. He felt that the industry had turned the art of music into "an entertainment process; a means, not an end; a medium, not a message. Music has lost its soul." His own family background and early playing days had been conducted in the atmosphere of community activity, where music had a meaning and a "soul". His parents were Jehovah's Witnesses. Perhaps the spiritual and religious element, dominant in his performing and writing, stems from this. He perceives that:

> this music that came out of gospel and blues and hillbilly music has developed into something that is rootless . . . some of us have to put some of the threads together to make it real – to put some reality into it.[3]

He admitted in a 1982 interview that he hadn't really "rated" Irish music in Belfast when he was young. He has since come to an opposite view.

> I think it can be dangerous to not validate the music of where you're from, for anybody . . . For me it's traditional. I'm a traditionalist. I believe in tracing things back to the source and finding out what the real thing was, and how it changed.

Beautiful Vision, released in 1982, came as a consequence of this first journey back to the Celtic homeland. It integrated folk and rhythm and blues idioms, embracing traditional music through the use of uilleann pipes in "Celtic Ray". "Cleaning Windows" is an affectionate hymn to his youth and musical roots in Belfast. The traditional mood was heightened on the next album, *Inarticulate Speech of the Heart*. Here he made use of uilleann pipes and acoustic instrumentation on "Celtic Swing", while the jaunty "Connswater" is inhabited by the spirit of Irish march music.

Inarticulate Speech of the Heart was followed in 1985 by *A Sense of Wonder*. The Irish trad/rock band The Moving Hearts contributed one track, "Boffyflow and Spike", and piper Davy

---

[3] Van Morrison to Dermot Stokes, *Hot Press,* Vol. 6, No. 6, 1 April, 1982.

Spillane played on the title track. *No Guru, No Method, No Teacher* was released in 1986. This time Morrison included two songs on the exile theme: "One Irish Rover" and "Got to go Back".

The culmination of his love affair with Irish music resulted in the *Irish Heartbeat* album. One critic exclaimed: "Van Morrison has publicly laid his Celtic music cards on the table, making explicit what has long been implicit in his music." In this album he collaborated with the traditional group The Chieftains. *Irish Heartbeat* is his interpretation of mainly folk material like "The Star of the County Down", a bouncy Northern song on which Morrison sang and played drums; "My Lagan Love", a haunting and beautiful modal air which has a difficult melodic progression; and "On Raglan Road", a song associated with another great Irish singer of ballads, the late Luke Kelly. On the old Belfast street song "I'll Tell Me Ma", another Clancy Brothers favourite, Morrison's lusty performance delivered complete with Belfast intonation reclaims a Northern spirit. When the album was released he remarked to one interviewer:

> Now you get all these crossovers. People have to make connections because in this modern age we live in, which is the video age, you're allowed five minutes. You have to make more connections than that, otherwise you're gonna starve.

Unforgettable Fire: U2

Undoubtedly the most important rock band to come out of Ireland and feature on the world stage is U2. Formed in 1976 when the band members were still schoolboys, U2 achieved the dizzy heights of the cover of Rolling Stone magazine by 1985. The distinctive U2 style, developed over the years, is loud and raw, characterised by the huge voice and impassioned lyrics of Paul Hewson, better known as Bono, and the guitar sound of Dave Evans, nicknamed The Edge.

Bono's lyrics range from political and social issues like American imperialism, heroin addiction, human rights violations and war, to more personal songs of love and relationships. The band has been associated for many years with causes like Amnesty International, CND and Live Aid.

Musically the band was committed to an exploration of the roots of rock 'n' roll, as was evident in the album *Rattle and Hum*. U2 differed from other aspiring Irish rock bands in that it set its sights on America rather than Britain. Bono drew from American musical and lyrical inspiration. It was, after all, "the birthplace of rock 'n' roll". Out of this involvement with American music Bono discovered his Irish identity. It came as a revelation to him that Irish music had contributed to rock 'n' roll. He sees the ballad as playing a crucial role in that contribution and this is where his notion of Irishness is rooted. The Irish component in his work is "the tradition of the story-teller that comes across". As for performance:

> the Irish are less uptight about what's inside them, therefore they let it out easier and it comes out in a raw way and that's very like the spirit of black music and gospel music.

Bob Dylan has been a major influence. It surprised Bono to find that:

> Dylan talks about The Clancy Brothers, and the McPeakes and how much he was
> influenced by Irish music. He sees it as a central and formative influence on his own work.
> That blew my mind when he told me this because I'd never thought of him in that way.

Bono had rejected all aspects of Irish music and culture when he was at school.

> I rebelled against being Irish, I rebelled against speaking the Irish language, Irish culture . . .
> Batman, Robin, Superman – that was more part of my experience than Finn McCool and
> the legends and mythology of Ireland.

Something of Irish culture did manage to penetrate this attitude. One of his teachers introduced him
to the music of Seán Ó Riada which, despite himself, he liked. Then in 1973 Thin Lizzy had a hit with
the old Clancy Brothers song "Whiskey in the Jar". "In fact, I think one of the first things I ever played
on acoustic guitar was 'Whiskey in the Jar', but that was before the electric version came out."

He was on "a voyage of self-discovery" through Irish music during the eighties. He found
himself drawn to "the pure . . . poetic spirit of an instrument like the uilleann pipes". At the same time
he grappled with the problem of Irish identity in the late twentieth century: "The confusion over my

own identity and the group's identity is part of the reason why I [was] digging into Irish folk music and the ballad form." He felt strongly that U2 was a rock band which was indigenous, and was Irish.

> I think there's an Irishness to what U2 do; I'm not quite sure what it is. I think it's something to do with the romantic spirit of the words I write, but also of the melodies that Edge makes on the guitar. Now the rock 'n' roll element that comes through [drummer] Larry Mullen would hardly be Irish, yet the abandonment in the way he plays the kit is intrinsically Irish.

This feeling for and exploration of Irish balladry and music will continue to be reflected in his songwriting:

> I think . . . Irish music reminds us of the humanity that we're losing, of a past that we all share. It's a common past and Irish music is a part of it.

Sinéad O'Connor

Reams have been written about the singer Sinéad O'Connor more on account of her turbulent public persona than about her work. This has tended to obscure the distinction between the life and the work more than is usual, even in a celebrity driven age such as this.

A precociously early start in the music business came about at age fourteen when she provided the vocal track on a first single released by the Irish band In Tua Nua. Released on the prestigious Island label, this led on to a short stint with another fledging Irish band. This ended when she was signed to record an album of her own material and the trajectory of her career path was thus plotted out. Her album *The Lion and the Cobra* appeared in 1987 when she was nineteen, a prodigious achievement for such a young singer-songwriter. On the strength of its success she became a star and has remained ever since an emblematic, though troubled, figure in Irish music and in Irish public life.

Now 32, O'Connor has built up a steady rather than voluminous output of albums of which 1989's *I do not want what I haven't got* achieved the widest acclaim. It included the track "Nothing Compares To U", which was a global Number 1. For that album also she recorded a version of the song "I am Stretched on your Grave", unaccompanied save for a minimal drum backing. The words are a translation by the Irish poet Frank O'Connor of a twelfth-century poem in Irish, "Ta Mé Sínte Ar Do Thuama" ("I am stretched on your grave"), set to music by singer Philip King and recorded by him in 1979. The air is a composition in the Sean Nós, or unaccompanied, style. In its older Irish language form it was recorded for *Bringing It All Back Home* by the late Diarmuid Ó Súilleabháin of Cúil Aodha.

For O'Connor, vocals have always been paramount. Both in performance and in recordings she has marked her preference for unaccompanied singing, which comes straight out of the sung tradition in both Irish and English. Her vocal technique and her dynamic range bear signs of the folk influence.

While she has publicly rejected the idea of Ireland as anything other than a modern twentieth-century society, her choice of material and singing style belie this. The vocal influences, particularly the emphasis on the solo voice, are Irish and pre-pop. "I am Stretched on your Grave" is frequently mistaken for "the real thing", an Irish traditional song. Sinéad's father, who was an accomplished tenor in the Irish style, taught her Irish songs and ballads when she was a child. Nowadays the folk and "Celtic" elements are still there, mixed with rap, funk and other elements of contemporary music.

Mainstream rock is a given of Irish music, as are all its hybrids and offshoots which flourish in global music culture everywhere. Dance, house, hip hop, acid jazz, garage, metal, and so on are trans-national vernaculars. The effectiveness of mass media information technology and global capitalism will ensure that this will continue to be so. Big audiences and big markets cluster around all these varieties of contemporary styles. Most do not connect with indigenous music in Ireland but some of the best of the Irish bands, from U2 to the Corrs, have taken inspiration, wittingly or otherwise, from the great store of singing and instrumental music that makes up the Irish tradition. Whether it is in the lyrical spirit, or the performance, or the actual cadences of the music itself, it is present and undeniable.

Siblings The Corrs are an international hit playing modern music peppered with traditional sound.

Twelve

No Frontiers: Irish Music since the Seventies

Traditional music has a place in contemporary music because it can still be itself, still be alive and not affect the ongoing tradition of source music.

DÓNAL LUNNY

New Folk

Seventies Ireland was a creative environment for folk and traditional music and for its offshoots and hybrids. It was a time of music festivals and independent record labels with agenda other than the purely commercial. The vibrant music scene was a reflection of the general mood of the country when, for the first time ever, Irish emigrants were returning home to live. Ireland boasted the youngest population in Europe and Irish music had a bigger audience than ever before.

The decade produced some outstanding bands and several prominent solo artists. Many, though not all, of those bands have since broken up, but most of the musicians are still performing. The creative interaction between diverse musical forms – traditional, folk, blues, country and rock – had long-term consequences for the future development of contemporary music in Ireland.

Planxty

Although they played traditional material, most of the seventies' bands had few members who came from the "pure" tradition, i.e. had grown up playing orally transmitted music. This was true of Planxty, one of the most important and innovative bands of this time. Only one of its members, the piper Liam O'Flynn, fell into the category of traditional musician. Like most young Irish people, the others had grown up listening to rock 'n' roll and pop music. They had come to traditional music via the folk revival of the sixties.

The instigator of Planxty (the name comes from a title for a type of seventeenth-century harp tune) was Christy Moore. Moore returned to Ireland in the early seventies, having worked the folk-club circuit in the U.K. He invited Andy Irvine and Dónal Lunny to make up the four-piece which within months of its formation made a profound impression on both Irish music fans and other musicians.

The band produced an identifiable "Planxty sound" almost immediately, made up of Moore's unique vocal style and personality, innovative tune arrangements and uniformly high quality playing and singing. Instrumental music featuring O'Flynn's piping was a major component in the sonic identity of the band and O'Flynn was an important source of tunes from the tradition. The guitar, bouzouki and mandolin accompaniment was unlike anything heard before in traditional music ensemble playing; Lunny and Irvines' technical mastery of their instru-

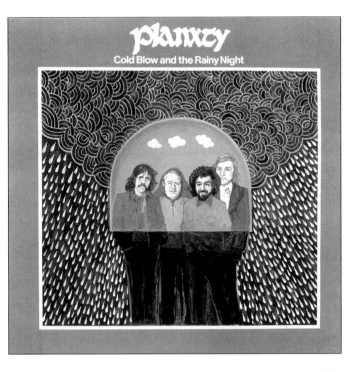

ments, plus highly original arrangements of tunes and songs, set down the parameters for ensemble playing for years to come.

Lunny, who had grown up in Newbridge, County Kildare – Moore's home town – was drawn into traditional music by chance. An interest in rock 'n' roll led him towards the guitar. The only opportunity to play was in local pubs where traditional musicians used to meet: "There weren't a lot of guitars around so I had a free rein . . . that's where I became properly involved in traditional music. I wasn't really thinking about what I was doing." Accompaniment in Irish traditional music is problematic and Lunny was aware that it was essentially an unaccompanied form, but:

> I've always had strong feelings that the music should be expanded and added to in the same way as contemporary music because people actually miss that; people find . . . unaccompanied music too intense in a modern context; people are used to hearing a rhythm section, used to hearing a bass.

With Planxty he remembered there was a personally decisive moment. It came during a recording he was making with Liam O'Flynn.

> I ended up after several hours playing a drone on a bouzouki, and what I was coming round to was that the tune was at its purest and its best without accompaniment. I mentally painted myself into a corner . . . and it took me the rest of the day to get out of that, but

it was a matter of making a decision on what way I was going to go . . . I remember making the decision that I accompany music, and Irish music can be accompanied without affecting its character.

This decision effectively shaped Lunny's career and has marked his work as a musician, arranger, and composer ever since.

Planxty's sources for songs were other singers, especially traditional singers, and old song collections. The search for songs led them back to the places where the oral tradition was still alive. Moore and Irvine were constantly seeking out songs and singers and both amassed huge collections of material in this way. For many of those in the audience at a Planxty gig, it was their first encounter with songs like "Little Musgrave" or "Ye Rambling Boys of Pleasure" which led them back to the "pure" tradition. With Planxty there was an agenda to present the material in a way which would make sense in contemporary cultural terms.

Lunny recalled: "Everybody cared so much about the music and about the songs; I think unconsciously we were all trying to do definitive versions."

One of their departures from standard practice was to segue from a vocal number into a traditional dance tune. This was Moore's idea:

There was a huge gap between people's consciousness of Irish traditional music and people's awareness of Irish singing. Irish folk songs were sung all over the country, but traditional music wasn't played all over the country – it was happening at little sessions in pubs.

It was also through the band's innovative use of the bouzouki that this instrument has become almost mandatory in traditional music accompaniment. Adapted to accommodate western chords by the addition of a fourth set of strings and given a flat back, it now has become a standard in the instrumentation of Irish traditional music. Initially introduced into Ireland by Johnny Moynihan, an early member of Planxty, it was adopted by Lunny, Irvine, and De Dannan's Alec Finn (who plays the Greek, six-stringed version with rounded back and original tunings). Lunny preferred bouzouki to guitar for accompanying traditional

Left: Dónal Lunny;
Right: Alec Finn of
De Dannan, with
daughter Heather.

The Dubliners

music: "It's a bit emptier and didn't tend to fill the music or to colour the music as strongly as the guitar . . . It has become an individual element of Irish music, which is no bad thing."

Planxty split up in 1975, reformed in 1978, and went on to make three further albums, before finally deciding to call it a day in 1981 when Moore and Lunny left to form the contemporary jazz/rock driven Moving Hearts.

The Dubliners

Around 1963 (even the band is not quite sure when it came about) the Dubliners were formed. On first appearances they could have been mistaken for "just" a ballad group but, unlike many groups of the day, they boasted one, and later two, accomplished traditional players, banjo player Barney Mc Kenna and fiddler John Sheehan. Their singers, Ronny Drew and Luke Kelly, were unorthodox, both in their singing and appearance. Both of them sang in the raw, hard vocal style associated with street singers: the band had "street cred" before the term was invented. Against the tweeness of wholesome vocalising and sweet harmonies favoured by some ballad singers, the Dubliners stood for the authentic sound of the tradition.

Compelling and intense in live performance, Luke Kelly possessed an enormous voice but, sadly, died in his forties. He was a committed human rights activist whose choice of material reflected his political opinions and identification with working-class issues. Songs like "McAlpines Fusiliers" and "The Hot Asphalt", which dealt with the experiences of Irish navvies in England, were typical of the material which attracted him.

John Sheehan described the Dubliners' approach as:

> Uninhibited . . . Ronny sang with a most peculiar voice, he didn't apologise to anybody for the way he sang, this was the voice that he found himself speaking with, and that's the way he sang . . . Luke was a unique singer . . . he had a great way of tackling a song and great phrasing and pacing.

There was a balance struck by the Dubliners between traditional music which had a rural root, and the songs, which tended more towards urban folk. Despite the folk and trad tag, there was something gritty and urban about the Dubliners. They sang work songs, rebel songs, bawdy songs, street songs, love songs and contemporary ballads.

In McKenna's opinion, folk music offered more to people in the sixties than, say, rock 'n' roll or pop:

> At that time most of the rock music was all "He and She" . . . it was all the one theme, you know what I mean; whereas the folk theme brought out a wider spectrum. You had songs and tunes about every walk in life.

In 1967 the Dubliners recorded "Seven Drunken Nights", which they had learned from Sean Nós singer Joe Heaney. Bawdy, suggestive and irreverent (although tame in comparison to today's standards of lyrical excess), it went into the British charts. This necessitated an appearance by the band on BBC television's "Top of the Pops", the first time that this kind of group or material had featured on the show.

Twenty years later they made another appearance on the same programme, this time in the company of The Pogues with whom they had recorded "The Irish Rover". This staple of boozy sing-songs and stage-Irishry was restored to its original chaotic comic state by the two groups and it, too, went into the charts in the U.K.

> The "Irish Rover" was recorded in about three or four hours; it was a case of "Right, what key is it in? We'll try G" . . . and just recorded it and that was it. There was no messing around for weeks and weeks like some of these pop groups, you know, on thousands of pounds.

McKenna attributed the band's long years of popular success to "our general attitude to life . . . it's the ease of pace; there's no mad panic at any stage . . . our popularity had something to do with the way we presented the whole thing. We stood up and here we were, take us or leave us".

Celtic Folkweave

Planxty and the Dubliners presented two different but complementary faces of Irish folk music. Planxty experimented with song arrangements, instrumentation and accompaniment. They looked for new ways to present old material (even though contemporary folk songs were always included). The Dubliners' traditional arrangements did not stray from standard presentation, but their singing style was unique, as were their collective and individual personalities.

The renewed interest in traditional and folk music in the seventies produced a slew of new bands, both traditional and contemporary folk. It was also the heyday of folk festivals, the most memorable at Ballisodare in County Sligo and Lisdoonvarna in County Clare. These were open-air events which took place over a weekend in the summer. There was also an international folk festival circuit, mainly in northern Europe: Germany, Switzerland, Denmark and France. They catered for the large numbers of continental Europeans interested in folk and traditional music. Many of them travelled to Ireland to attend concerts, festivals and sessions, or simply to be in the place where traditional music was "happening".

The European demand for Irish music made professional players out of many Irish musicians, traditional and otherwise. Part of the attraction of the European circuit of festivals, concerts and clubs was the prospect of meeting up with other musicians. The after-gig sessions were often looked forward to more than the gig itself.

The Supergroups

The seventies was the decade of the touring Irish traditional bands, the so-called "supergroups". Ó Riada's early work in the sixties with the proto-typical Ceoltóirí Chualann paved the way for professional group playing. Paddy Moloney, the piper of Ceoltóirí Chualann, went on to form The Chieftains with some members from that band. Nearly forty years on, The Chieftains remain the most well-known, successful and prolific of Irish traditional music ensembles. They also retain a strong traditional profile, although their recent recordings have been markedly collaborative across genres and other ethnic music traditions. Most memorable of these are *Irish Heartbeat* with Van Morrison, *Long Black Veil* with various rock musicians, and their most recent album of traditional songs sung by well-known women singers from the popular music world, *Tears From Stone*.

One of the most long-lived and popular bands on the European touring circuit was Clannad, a family group from the Irish-speaking area of Donegal in the north-west of the country. Máire, Pól and Ciarán Brennan grew up in Gaoth Dobhair, their mother's birthplace, and formed the band with close relatives Padraig and Noel O'Dúgáin while they were still in school. Their father, Leo Brennan, had run a dance band in the fifties and sixties and had involved the children in it when they were young. They were familiar through their mother with traditional songs in Irish and with popular music through their father, radio and records. Máire was also a classically trained musician, who played the modern Irish harp.

Clannad's music combined Irish traditional songs, in Irish, with jazz, classical, and folk idioms. The used no traditional instruments except for the bodhrán and harp, and included such foreigners as double bass, silver flute, and bongos. They developed a distinctive sound with this instrumentation, but also from their unique vocal settings of Donegal songs. They toured very successfully in Europe for several years, gradually developing into a folk rock band with jazz and classical overtones.

"Texture" was a key component of Clannad's sound. This was made possible by sound recording technology and achieved using synthesisers and extensive voice-over dubbing. This was the dominant element in their presentation, on record and in performance. The effect was moody, ethereal and atmospheric. The strangeness was enhanced by the sound of their Irish dialect (Donegal Gaelic). By the 1990s this mystical quality was the one which came to be seized upon as the identifying feature not only of Clannad's music but of "Celtic" music *per se*, "Celtic music" of course being wholly an invention of music industry niche marketers. Ironically, an effect which was only made possible by relatively recent developments in sound recording technology has been made to represent all that is supposed to be traditional in music in the heavily marketed package directed at today's Irish music consumers.

In 1982 Clannad were commissioned to write a theme for the TV series *Harry's Game*. The single released as a result reached number five in the British charts, the first song in Irish ever to do so. When Bono of U2 heard "Harry's Game" one day on his car radio, he was struck by the contrasting influences at work in the band. He admired the way Clannad married the "technology of the modern recording studio to the fragility and frailty of the human voice. And yet they're working with samplers and highly sophisticated keyboards and synthesisers, so I think that bodes well for the future of Irish music." In 1986 Bono and Clannad collaborated on the "Once in a Lifetime" single. Bono's powerful voice worked well as a foil for Máire's delicate vocals. This collaboration and Clannad's subsequent work in writing for film broadened their audience base. In 1990 Máire noted:

> There's been a huge change in our audience, and I suppose it goes right across the board with all the kinds of music we have touched on . . . but it's great to see the young people that you'd never see coming to a Clannad gig, now coming and really enjoying what we're doing, especially the Gaelic songs. Because they hear the wonderful melodies, and you actually hear English bands, new English bands using Irish melodies as well because they're gorgeous and they're very strong.

Enya

In 1992 a U.S. networked commercial for Volkswagen cars used Clannad's original recording of "Harry's Game". This gave the group massive coverage in the U.S. The resulting surge of interest in the group launched a second career lasting a number of years. These days Máire's energies are focussed on solo work and song writing, while the other members of the band are also pursuing other interests.

Máire's sister Enya, who was a member of Clannad for three years in the early eighties, went on to develop a hugely successful career as a solo recording artist, with record sales to date of more than thirty-three million. Enya's music is perhaps the definitive New Age soundtrack, incorporating all the elements associated in the consumer's mind with "Celtic music". Significantly, her first album, *Enya*, featured music written and produced for the BBC series "The Celts".

The vocal successes of Clannad in the seventies were equalled on the instrumental level by a new group, The Bothy Band. Planxty had disbanded in 1975, releasing Christy Moore to pursue a solo career. Dónal Lunny, meanwhile, joined The Bothy Band. Within a short time of its establishment it became the most popular traditional band in the country. Where Planxty had had a pronounced bias towards song, The Bothy Band's arrangements and performances of instrumental music were never less than memorable.

There were six players, three of whom were "pure", traditional players. These were Matt Molloy on flute, Paddy Keenan on pipes and Kevin Burke (preceded by Tommy Peoples) on fiddle. All

Frankie Gavin of De Dannan.

of these players remain in the front ranks of top class traditional players today. Of the remaining three, Dónal Lunny played bouzouki and bodhrán, Mícheál Ó Domhnaill played guitar and sang, as did his sister Triona, who also played clavinet. Lunny described the "Bothies" as:

> six people lashing away at the tunes . . . That was the one thing which it was famous for; it was very fast and furious playing . . . there was more emphasis on traditional tunes and there were more possibilities for arranging the music because of the fact that there were six players.

The Bothies' arrangements, choice of tunes and their way of playing set the standard for much ensemble playing in later years. Lunny's use of the bouzouki as a rhythm instrument attracted many imitators. He describes his style as "a combination of harmonies and rhythm and a certain amount of counterpoint".

The bouzouki features in another Irish supergroup that came together in the seventies, namely the Galway-based band De Dannan. While De Dannan has had several first-rate singers over the years, it is famous for its driving, energetic style and melodic arrangements of dance tunes. The two core members are fiddle player Frankie Gavin and bouzouki player and guitarist Alec Finn. Together they developed a recognisable "De Dannan sound": fast, melodic fiddle set off by distinctive counter harmonies on bouzouki, and accompanied by cello, bodhrán, flute and button accordion. Traditional dance music is the core element in De Dannan's repertoire, although they have enjoyed much popular success through their song recordings. They have also taken excursions into other styles and idioms. The band once recorded an instrumental version of the Beatles song "Hey Jude" which they managed to transpose into a credible set of Irish dance tunes. This was followed in subsequent years by traditional interpretations of classical tunes, another Beatles song, Jewish Klezmer music and black gospel music.

The group were recorded in New York for *Bringing It All Back Home* playing a traditional set, with the Donna Brown Gospel Singers from Harlem, and a set with Jewish Klezmer musician Andy Statman. Statman heard about De Danann through his involvement with an Irish recording company in New York. In their music he detected similarities to Klezmer, which he described as "the instrumental music of the Jews of Eastern Europe".

"There is an obvious relationship superficially . . . in the phrasing and in the ornamentation . . . both are very highly ornamented forms, and some of the ornaments are the same."

Out of this relationship came some new tunes for De Dannan: "The Jewish Reels", "The Flatbush Waltz" and "The Shepherd's Dream". The tone and attack of the best Klezmer is well matched to the De Dannan style.

Fundamentally, De Dannan remain committed to the "roots" of Irish traditional music, and in particular to the memory of great players like Coleman, Morrison, Killoran and McKenna. For Frankie Gavin this connection is very important because

> those were the people who knew how to play the music as far as I'm concerned; those are the only recordings that we have where we can get an idea of what the music really sounded like in those days, and they were certainly producing the goods.

De Danann's singers have included Mary Black, Dolores Keane, Maura O'Connell, Elanor Shanley and Tommy Fleming, each of whom has gone on to a successful solo career.

New Directions – Paul Brady

One Irish musician whose career has woven in and out of traditional, folk and rock 'n' roll is Paul Brady. Like Dónal Lunny, Brady's first musical influences were rock 'n' roll. While a student in Dublin in the mid-

Since the eighties, after some years singing traditional and folk material, Mary Black has enjoyed a flourishing career as a contemporary singer. Her singing retains its traditional inflection and her choice of materials tends to the ballad idiom. For *Bringing It All Back Home* she recorded a song appropriately entitled "No Frontiers", from her album of the same name. The song was written by Jimmy MacCarthy, who has been a one-man song writing industry for Irish singers since the early eighties. An accomplished singer and player himself, MacCarthy recorded an album of his own compositions called *Song of the Singing Horseman*, which also featured "No Frontiers". MacCarthy is a ballad writer *par excellence*, distilling from the older form a contemporary resonance in shape and content.

Dolores Keane also made the transition to solo artist. Keane comes from a family of traditional singers in County Galway. For *Bringing It All Back Home* she wore two hats, that of the traditional singer with her aunts Sarah and Rita, and that of the contemporary performer, singing Mick Hanley's song about Irish emigration in the nineties, "My Love is in America".

Country music star Emmylou Harris singing with Dolores Keane and Mary Black in Nashville, Tennessee.

sixties, he played in several young rhythm-and-blues and rock 'n' roll bands. He met Lunny and Mick Moloney around this time and through them came into contact with folk and traditional music. In 1967 he joined Moloney in The Johnstons and made a thirteen-year commitment to traditional and folk music. For much of this time he was based in England (for more on this period of his life, see Chapter Ten).

The Johnstons' repertoire was comprised of traditional ballads and contemporary folk songs. They had a successful career until their demise in 1974. Brady places The Johnstons right at the head of the folk revival in Ireland: "I think that The Johnstons were really the first group . . . to bring Irish singing to the population of Ireland since the Clancy Brothers."

In 1974 Brady returned to Ireland to join Planxty. At this stage he says he went "digging for lots of songs . . . I was still primarily interested in being a traditional performer, a traditional singer, finding folk songs". The year after Planxty broke up in 1975, Brady and his Planxty colleague Andy Irvine joined forces and produced an album of folk songs.

The *Andy Irvine/Paul Brady* album contained traditional songs collected by Brady and Irvine and arrangments including a variety of "new" folk instruments, such as bouzouki, mandolin and cittern. The superb vocal arrangements and harmonies achieved by the pair made this album a classic and one which is still in demand.

Andy Irvine and Paul Brady performing in the seventies.

Both of them collected songs at source, that is, from singers in the traditional (solo and unaccompanied) style. Brady, in particular, collected many songs from singers of his part of the country around County Tyrone in Northern Ireland, where there is a very strong singing tradition.

In 1978 Brady made his last traditional album, *Welcome Here Kind Stranger*. With this album, which included one of his most popular songs, "The Lakes of Ponchartrain", he felt he had gone as far as he could go with traditional and folk idioms, both in terms of arrangements and technically. He believed that there was a side of his creative imagination that was not being expressed in folk and traditional music.

> I was finding parts of myself that were just new, so I found in me a need to express this and to write songs . . . I also wanted to get back into playing rock music.

In the space of a year he made a complete about-turn. In 1981 he released a rock album featuring his own songs and an electric band. In the intervening twenty years he has continued to work in this idiom, but he does not feel that he has left traditional music behind entirely:

> I think that the whole experience of Irish music and the falling in love with songs made me want to become a songwriter, and when I saw people in America, like Bob Dylan, were also coming out of that tradition . . . that made me feel that I could start to do that, too.

Although he can isolate several musical strains in his own work, one is pre-eminent: "What comes out . . . is that Irish voice with Irish inflections, with Irish accent, with Irish melodies. I think it will always be the main thing in what I am."

CROSSOVER

Paul Brady made a complete break with traditional music in 1981. Dónal Lunny also wanted to break out of the traditional mainstream, but did not want to leave it behind. The Bothy Band had broken up in 1979, leaving him free to engage with what had become a dominant musical preoccupation – that of the possibility of merging rock and traditional idioms in music instrumentation and arrangement.

> My interest at this time was applying [a rock rhythm section] to Irish music, maintaining an Irishness, if you like, to the style of music we were playing. It was extremely difficult for me to do this. However, we did eventually figure out a way to play traditional tunes which I think held on to most of their personality and character.

Moving Hearts, set up in 1981 by Christy Moore and Dónal Lunny, was the vehicle. Moore wanted to present contemporary Irish songs in a way which would be equally reflective both of the contemporary and the Irish; Lunny felt that this was compatible with his rock aspirations for traditional music.

Aside from Moore on vocals, Moving Hearts leaned heavily towards the instrumental. There was a saxophone player, a piper, bass and lead guitarists, drums and percussion, and Lunny on a range of instruments, electric and acoustic bouzouki, and synthesisers. From its earliest days the band's attempt to make this connection between traditional music and electric rock was met with universal approval. Moving Hearts won a huge following amongst young people around the country. Their gigs were typically hot and steamy affairs, heavy on dance and rhythm, vocally strong and musically about the most interesting thing going in the area of crossover. Unfortunately, Moving Hearts was too big to be economically viable and was forced to disband in 1984. The last album, *The Storm*, recorded in 1985 posthumously, so to speak, was exclusively instrumental. According to Lunny it revealed "a quality which hadn't been as apparent before . . . I think the band actually came into its own for the first time with the instrumental music that we played".

After the band broke up Christy Moore went on to develop a solo career which brought him to the forefront of Irish public life as an entertainer and performer, but also as a mordant critic of Irish society, outspoken in his commitment to issues like prisoner rights, Travellers, and the anti-nuclear movement. His recent departure from live performance and extensive touring has removed one of the country's best loved and most popular entertainers from the scene.

Many Irish artists and bands who find themselves working in non-traditional genres "speak with an Irish voice". Luka Bloom left Ireland in the eighties to restart a flagging career as a singer-songwriter and met with success in America. In the New York sessions for *Bringing It All Back Home* he sang two songs, both of which bear upon Ireland in different ways. "You couldn't have come at a Better Time" takes its opening melody line from an Irish dance tune, "The Kesh Jig", which was popularised by The Bothy Band in the seventies. Bloom was accompanied on the recording by New York traditional fiddler Eileen Ivers. For this recording she played what was to become her trademark instrument, a bright blue electric fiddle.

    "This is for Life" has no discernible Irish musical base, but it has a strong Irish connection. It is the story of two lovers, one Irish, one American, who "transcend the system which separates them". Both songs are contemporary.

> I don't come from a romantic Ireland, I come from a totally
> contemporary . . . modern Ireland with all its problems, and
> that's the Ireland I sing about, if I sing about Ireland at all.

Luka Bloom recording
in Hoboken, New Jersey.

The Irish accent, then, can be in the musical or substantive construction, or both. For Irishman Pierce Turner, it's in the melody and the singing style. Turner is based in New York but is a frequent visitor to Ireland. From musical beginnings, which included a stint in a show band, he progressed to the avant-garde milieu inhabited by musicians like Philip Glass. He is a singer-songwriter and recorded a song he calls "All Messed Up" for *Bringing It All Back Home*. The melody played on piano is constructed around a traditional Irish song, "Seán Ó Duibhir an Ghleanna", and the singing style is incantatory. This is not surprising; Turner cites Seán Ó Riada (who recorded this on his last album) and plainchant as two major influences on his development as a musician.

    "Cooler at the Edge", recorded by Scullion for *Bringing It All Back Home,* is a song about emigration, a theme very current in Irish songwriting in the eighties. Sonny Condell, songwriter and founder of Scullion, a contemporary band with a repertoire based on Condell's compositions, has been defiantly label resistant from its foundation. There was undoubtedly a strong folk influence and the band covered traditional songs in the early days. Scullion was one of the first of the new-wave bands of the seventies to combine instruments like saxophone and uilleann pipes.

Lunny continued to interrogate musical identities in new compositions and arrangements. He began to feel that Irish music was:

closer to African or oriental music than it is to American music . . . the punctuation of contemporary rhythms doesn't always suit Irish music.

One composition in which these relativities are worked through is "April 3rd", commissioned and recorded for *Bringing It All Back Home*. "April 3rd" is an instrumental piece whose melodic structure is based on Irish traditional music. Rhythm is a dominant voice in the composition. The instrumentation is a combination of electric and acoustic, including pipes, fiddle, keyboards, electric guitars, lead guitar played by The Edge (of U2), bouzouki, bodhrán, and timpani and percussion. The inclusion of several hand drums (bodhrán, Egyptian hand drum, and percussion section) reflects this. "April 3rd" is a tapestry of percussive "running rhythms" and melody.

The theme of "running rhythms" surfaces constantly in Lunny's work. In 1996, having spent some years working almost exclusively as a producer, he got together with another group of musicians to form the band Coolfin and release an album in 1998. Featuring Maighréad Ní Dhomhnaill (vocals), Nollaig Casey (fiddle), John McSherry (pipes), Sharon Shannon (box accordion), Ray Fean (drums), Graham Henderson (keyboards), Lyoyd Byrne (percussion) and Ronnie O'Flynn (bass), Coolfin was a contemporary trad juggernaut with gig firepower to equal any rock band. An optimist in all things, Lunny has always taken the view that change is a good thing for tradition.

Musicians who have learned traditional music or been involved with traditional music play it the way it should be played; they'll have an Irish accent that will come through any context . . .

Let's Dance

One of the undoubted cultural watersheds in Irish music in the nineties happened during the 1994 Eurovision Song Contest held in Dublin. Out of the blue, an intermission act entitled "Riverdance" received such a tumultuous reception from the audience that the (Irish) winning entry was almost eclipsed. It was also an instant hit with the millions who watched the show on television.

Michael Flately and
Jean Butler creating
a sensation in
"Riverdance".

Composer Bill Whelan, dancers Michael Flatley and Jean Butler, and the show's producers had set out to do for Irish dance what had been done with Irish music presentation in the sixties and seventies. Irish step dancing had become hidebound in terms of presentation and more or less confined to competition. Around the end of the eighties companies like Siamsa Tíre, the National Folk Theatre, had attempted to go the stage presentation route with Irish dance, as had groups like The Chieftains and Mick Moloney's band by incorporating dance routines into the show with some success.

It seemed as if Riverdance was waiting to happen. Composer Bill Whelan had previously worked as both a performer and producer with Planxty and had scored an intermission act for the band to play at the 1981 Eurovision Song Contest. Entitled "Timedance", this piece also involved dance, but from classical ballet rather than the step dance tradition. Riverdance, on the other hand, brought together virtuoso dancers from the competitive step dance tradition with both traditional and contemporary musicians. Around a theme of oppositions – male/female, river/earth, good/evil – Riverdance presented a panorama of ethnic music song and dance culture filtered through the lens of the modern spectacular stage show. Extended from seven minutes to a full hour and half show, Riverdance has toured extensively around the world and become a generic show, with three touring companies performing simultaneously.

Michael Flatley, whose background is that of first generation Irish-American with roots in the strong traditional dance and music culture of his parents, broke with the Riverdance company over intellectual copyright (a new issue in contemporary Irish music culture). He went on to to devise his own show, "Lord of The Dance", which has been as successful as its progenitor. Both shows and their touring companies have opened up the world of professional dance performance to skilled Irish step dancers and provide employment for professional Irish musicians of all disciplines at a level that would have been inconceivable in the eighties and before.

The trickledown effect has been a huge renewal of interest in and radical change in presentation of the dance. Both shows feature traditional musicians, but not traditional music as such, and it is the dance routines which are at the heart of the show. The status of Irish step dancing has undoubtedly benefited from the high profile and dance schools worldwide have seen a huge upturn in numbers coming to classes.

The Branding of Irish Music

The folk music revival of the sixties and seventies had significant spin-offs for the tourism industry, emanating from the marketing of Irish pubs and Irish music as two sides of the same Irish coin. In this scheme of things the Irish pub was portrayed as the most significant milieu in which Irish music culture was carried on; in fact, the pub was a relative latecomer in Irish traditional music practice. Music was not universally tolerated in Irish pubs prior to the sixties and the widespread practice of excluding women from pubs in Ireland did not totally die out until the eighties in some places. Pub sessions were well established by the late sixties, but these were generally spontaneous, unpaid and unscheduled events held entirely at the discretion of the players. This aspect of Irish traditional music practice has been almost totally commercialised to the detriment of the music.

The association of traditional music and pubs further obscures the rationale behind playing music in the first place. More often than not it is the commercial imperative, that of selling drink, which makes traditional music a marketing tool for the beverage and tourism industries. The music itself is a secondary consideration. Companies sponsor traditional music events, the performance of which is inevitably bound up with drink consumption and product placement. Traditional musicians increasingly find themselves struggling to be heard in noisy pubs, competing against ringing tills and conversation. Themed "Irish pubs" proliferate outside the country from Beijing to Zurich, complete with "authentic" Irish décor, staff and, of course, music. These are places where the customer is a kind of virtual tourist and where an "image" of Ireland and "Irishness" is presented out of which a market for Irish culture is cultivated, a brand is born.

This presents a challenge to Irish culture in general but most critically to music, which is in the front line. Thus far it has been largely successful in its efforts to engage with the commercial world on its own terms, principally by offering alternatives to the "music as cultural product" model. Many traditional musicians, for example, are being drawn back to seated gigs and to venues where music can be listened to, where audience and player can be joint participants, and where the atmosphere allows for the music to extend itself across its full expressive range.

Irish traditional music has further consolidated itself around specific concerns in ways which will determine its development for the foreseeable future. Music education in particular made rapid advances in the nineties and centres of excellence and teaching institutions at all levels have achieved quite remarkable penetration throughout the country. There is still a big voluntary component in the teaching particularly of children through the Comhaltas organisation and other groups and this augurs well for the future of amateur music-making in the country. The growing network of *fleadhanna, feiseanna*, competitions, summer schools, seminars and so on reflects a high level of demand for music-related activities of all kinds, as does the welter of web sites and Internet activity based around Irish traditional music.

Irish traditional music made the transition from rural to urban, and from the agricultural milieu to the technological. Its resilience over the years has meant that it is singularly well adapted to accommodate change. Whether on the Internet or in the pub, concert hall, stadium, university, or kitchen, it sustains a global community of players and listeners. The facility with which it negotiates between change and continuity will maintain its equilibrium in years to come.

Photograph Credits

All photographs © BBC/Stephen Meaney, except:

Index